Praise for Harnessing the Dynamics of Public Education

"Schools evolve to meet the demands placed upon them by laws, legislatures, and culture. The result has been the unimaginative standardized educational processes that punish innovation and creativity. Drs. Timothy B. Jones and David C. Barrett's new book, *Harnessing the Dynamics of Public Education: Preparing for a Return to Greatness*, provides an important, and often critical, view of education. We must face what we have become before we can get better, but fortunately, there is a path to the schools we want."—**Wesley D. Hickey**, EdD, chair department of educational leadership and policy studies, The University of Texas at Tyler

"In their book Jones and Barrett draw attention, critically and importantly, to the deleterious nature of standardization in American education. The authors are instructive in their argument that America as a democratic society is witnessing the slow erosion of intellectual excellence that has been the hallmark of American's educational system, and a mainstay of America's democratic way of life. The authors focus on the need to transform, rightly so, old patterns that have contributed to the destruction of public education. Argued in this book is the need to create America's schools anew, taking a new path to greatness for public education, shattering outdated and constrictive notions of traditions in favor of a new paradigm that permeates and gives way to thinking and necessary actions."—**Patrick M. Jenlink**, EdD, E.J. Campbell Endowed Chair in Educational Leadership, Stephen F. Austin State University

"In *Harnessing the Dynamics of Public Education*, the reader is immediately drawn into this book's story and premise. The authors skillfully establish not only the need for change in American education, they do so with bold words. Their use of seven drivers to return public education to greatness is clever and intellectually provocative. The reader cannot help but become motivated to join Drs. Jones and Barrett's call to return American public schools to their greatness."—**Lloyd Goldsmith**, EdD, professor and former principal, Abilene Christian University

"Inspiring and spot on! Drs. Jones and Barrett's new book provides hope and strategy for one of America's most important institutions returning to the prominence it deserves."—**Russell D. Marshall**, superintendent, Mabank Independent School District

"In *Harnessing the Dynamics of Public Education*, Drs. Jones and Barrett emphasize the importance of school improvement efforts in order to empower stakeholders to initiate needed school change. They stress the critical nature of saving public education and the vital role authentic leaders play in creating and maintaining effective and competitive campuses for the future. This should be a required read for practicing school leaders and those who prepare and certify them."—**Casey Graham Brown**, associate professor and chair, Department of Educational Leadership and Policy Studies, The University of Texas at Arlington

"*Harnessing the Dynamics of Public Education: Preparing for a Return to Greatness* is a wide-angle take on, and prescription for, the current state of America's school system. With great clarity and insight, the authors make a persuasive argument that in order for there to be authentic learning in schools, there must be authentic teaching. This requires a journey toward authentic leadership—that finding and pursuing your own authentic leadership in teaching—is the key to regaining quality education in our school systems. The future belongs to leaders who want to win, without ever losing track of their own values. We live in a day when the best people can work or learn anywhere. They will follow authenticity—a person who leads with passion and purpose." —**Michelle Cummings**, owner, Training Wheels Group LLC

"As educators it is easy to get caught up in the, 'it was good enough in the past/it is good enough for the present,' mentality. The students of today express their ideas in a different manner than students of the past, for instance, the way we did. Dr. Jones and Dr. Barrett skillfully articulate to the reader the importance of evolving as an educational system and making learning relevant for today's (and tomorrow's) learners." —**Terry Lapic**, superintendent, East Texas Charter High School and Calvin Nelms Charter School

"As a business owner I think this book offers hope for providing a future full of creative individuals and thinkers on a global scale through a personalized education versus a standardized process that doesn't address businesses needs for twenty-first-century skills." —**Ken Skaggs**, president/founder 3008 Editing & Audio

HARNESSING THE DYNAMICS OF PUBLIC EDUCATION

HARNESSING THE DYNAMICS OF PUBLIC EDUCATION

Preparing for a Return to Greatness

Timothy B. Jones and David C. Barrett

Foreword by James A. Vornberg

Rowman & Littlefield
Lanham • Boulder • New York • London

Published by Rowman & Littlefield
A wholly owned subsidiary of The Rowman & Littlefield Publishing Group, Inc.
4501 Forbes Boulevard, Suite 200, Lanham, Maryland 20706
www.rowman.com

Unit A, Whitacre Mews, 26-34 Stannary Street, London SE11 4AB

Copyright © 2016 by Timothy B. Jones and David C. Barrett

All rights reserved. No part of this book may be reproduced in any form or by any electronic or mechanical means, including information storage and retrieval systems, without written permission from the publisher, except by a reviewer who may quote passages in a review.

British Library Cataloguing in Publication Information Available

Library of Congress Cataloging-in-Publication Data
Jones, Timothy B.
  Harnessing the dynamics of public education : preparing for a return to greatness / Timothy B. Jones and David C. Barrett ; foreword by James A. Vornberg.
      pages cm
  Includes bibliographical references.
  ISBN 978-1-4758-0872-8 (cloth : alk. paper) — ISBN 978-1-4758-0873-5 (pbk. : alk. paper) — ISBN 978-1-4758-0874-2 (electronic) 1. Public schools—United States. 2. Education—United States. 3. Education—Aims and objectives—United States. 4. Educational change—United States. I. Title.
  LA217.2.J656 2016
  371.010973—dc23
                                                                    2015022696

∞™ The paper used in this publication meets the minimum requirements of American National Standard for Information Sciences—Permanence of Paper for Printed Library Materials, ANSI/NISO Z39.48-1992.

Printed in the United States of America

For every professional educator that has stepped out of the box or taken a chance to make a positive difference in the life of a child! You are a rare breed and absolutely critical for public education's return to greatness!

Other books by Timothy B. Jones

Education for the Human Brain: A Road Map to Natural Learning in Schools (2013)

Contents

Foreword	xi
Acknowledgments	xvii
Introduction: Harnessing the Dynamics of Public Education: Preparing for a Return to Greatness	1
1 Building a Naturally Great School	9
2 Fostering a New Mindset for the Future	25
3 The War on American Public Education	39
4 Comprehensive Accountability	53
5 Overcoming Pedagogical Paralysis	67
6 Authentic Leadership	85
7 The Price of Safety	99
8 The Return to Greatness	115
About the Authors	129

Foreword
James A. Vornberg

Public Education—A necessity for a Democratic Republic and World Leadership. As one looks over the past 250 years of history, not only of our nation but of the civilized world, there is a constant in the many factors that have played not only a significant but an increasing role. That constant is the need for education to keep the progress of civilization moving forward for the betterment of humanity. Every informed individual realizes the impact that education has had on a functioning nation and world over the past few centuries.

Thomas Jefferson was perhaps the American who first carried the torch nationally for the need of an educated population to ensure the continued means of moving both a nation and a civilization forward, especially if the means of maintaining its progress was to continue in the future. Jefferson called attention to this in his writings and also in his actions as his administration concluded the deal for the Louisiana Purchase and then sent the Corps of Discovery headed by Lewis and Clark off to explore the new holding. Jefferson had Lewis educated in the concepts of natural science that were then being used to understand the new resources that now belonged to this nation.

But Jefferson also knew that without an educated citizenry in the nation that was only about twenty-five years in existence, the democracy would not endure for the long term. There cannot be only an educated elite group of citizens that directs a republic, or it will fail. It takes a citizenry that understands the operation of science, democracy, the arts, and philosophy to maintain and change as needed so we continue as a nation to move forward both in a civilized manner and to meet the challenges of the future.

This philosophical ideal of Jefferson's that an educated citizenry was required was further developed by Thomas Mann who, after serving in the Massachusetts State House and then the state senate, became Secretary to the Massachusetts State Board of Education. This is where he demonstrated moral leadership by emphasizing pedagogy and having universal public-supported education for all students.

Every student, to remain in a free society, needed to be educated. Mann further supported that education needed to be moral in character but, also as a public offering, this must be free of sectarian religious influence and that schools should embrace students of all social, religious, and ethnic backgrounds. He helped to develop the idea that professional teachers would be well educated themselves and that educational methods used in the classroom would not include harsh practices that were often used during the early years of schools in the United States. Mann stated that these public schools would be supported and sustained financially, and controlled by a public that realized the importance of education for the good of all society.

Perhaps there is no better demonstration of the value of an education than the life of John Berry Meachum (1789–1854), who was born into slavery. By using his carpentry and barrel-making skills he eventually earned enough money to buy his freedom. He followed his enslaved wife when she was brought to St. Louis and bought her freedom as well. As his business success continued, he bought other slaves who paid him back by working for him. Because slaveholders of that time knew that an educated population was potentially a rebellious one, laws were made that prohibited the education of slaves.

Secretly Meachum operated a school in the basement of his church to educate African Americans in St. Louis. This protestant church was the first one to serve African Americans in that city and helped him educate a population that was being held hostage. Meachum's education opportunities helped them to survive as free men in a racist society. As one looks at the ideas that Jefferson spoke of, they are so well demonstrated in the story of John Berry Meachum: educated people understand what it is to remain free and responsible for their own support and well-being. When we, as a society, reduce our citizenry's opportunity for an adequate education, we only serve to harm our nation's opportunity to achieve those goals that are stated in the preamble of the U.S. Constitution:

> in order to form a more perfect union, establish justice, insure domestic tranquility, provide for the common defense, promote general welfare, and secure the blessings of liberty to ourselves and our posterity.

"It is better to support schools than jails." These words by Mark Twain capture perhaps one of the real and increasingly difficult issues of our time. Today it costs the public coffers tremendous amounts of money per person incarcerated—often more than it takes for an individual to live a middle-class life. Certainly it would cost much less to educate ten students during a year versus one prisoner.

The opportunity is great: to save money by helping change where we spend our public funds, and ultimately improve society, and to focus on the positive rather than the negative. Certainly where and how we spend public funds can have a gigantic impact on the future of our society and our country. When we consistently spend these funds on repairing people problems, but not affecting similar individuals before they become problem individuals to society, we are demonstrating that our nation, our state, and our local communities do not want to prepare for a better environment for its citizens.

Today there are many options for families to educate their children. We do not require our families to send their children to a school that is open to everyone. In fact, we have many options: private schools, religious schools, home schools, charter schools, alternative schools, magnet schools, virtual schools, special education schools, and early college high schools, in addition to the traditional public school.

Students and parents may choose to go to many of these schools, some of which require additional funds from the family. The important thing is that all children have the opportunity to go to a school that can prepare them for their future and the future of their nation. All students do not need to study at a school that has only a standardized curriculum.

Education is about preparing for a future that does not yet exist. Schools that do not open doors for discovery, experimentation, and understanding of how each student fits into an environment different from the present are not doing the job that needs to occur to maintain a developing and maturing nation and world. As Ken Robinson says, "Education doesn't need to be reformed—it needs to be transformed . . . to personalize it, to build achievement on discovering the individual talents of each child . . . and their true passions."

Toward what does all this point? It means that our educational systems must work toward creating students who are thinkers, better thinkers, thinkers who look to the future and not look back at the past. The changes are coming faster and faster in all areas of our environment. As a nation and as a world we have to become thinkers of the future and not thinkers of the past. We must see the new ideas that develop and determine how these can be helpful to affect our future by helping people to work together to solve the world's and the planet's problems.

When we only look to see how much wealth can be generated instead of seeing how the wealth we have can be made productive and supportive for our nation's growth and our world's cooperation, we will have failed for the long term, for our children and our great-grandchildren. So public schools make up a large part of the picture that will help us solve our issues and problems to achieve stability and progress in the world and nation.

Although there are other choices for education, most families and most communities depend on public schools to do this formal education. If public schools are not supported and continue to be developed for the common good, then our nation will not be able to compete for the leadership that we have been capable of offering our citizens for the last two hundred years.

This volume by Timothy Jones and David Barrett explores and develops the topic of how important and critical this need has become for our nation and searches the processes and paths that our leaders, both educationally and politically, need to take in continuing our nation's leadership to be at the forefront of progress for the future of the world. Every leader of our government—from the president of our nation to the local school board, from the Secretary of the Department of Education to our teachers in what was once called the common schools—must realize the significance of his or her role in this continuing search for maintaining the front edge of education for our nation.

Acknowledgments

A project this large obviously has many people behind the scenes whose contributions are significant. At the risk of leaving someone off this list, we wish to acknowledge the following individuals without whom this book could not have been successfully completed.

First, we want to thank Tom Koerner, vice president and editorial director at Rowman and Littlefield. Tom is a pleasure to work with and saw our vision of this work from the beginning. Elaine McGarraugh, our senior production editor (for the second time), and Carlie Wall, associate editor, were also invaluable in this process and whose professional work was obvious in the final product.

Obviously family is always involved in a project of this size whether it be directly or the many influences of a life together. We thank both of our sets of parents, Enoch and Gladys Jones and Steve and Mary Barrett for obviously instilling great value on education and supporting our work over the long term to make a difference as we stir things up. Jeffrey Jones and Adri Ruiz have supported us in so many specific and critical ways that clearly some of their voice is in our voice.

Noted scholar and great friend Jim Vornberg contributed the foreword to this book but has also been a mentor and colleague to both of us for many years. Jim teaches, mentors, inspires, and quite frankly helps in every way he can. His accomplishments as a scholar are too numerous to list and his commitment and care for his students and colleagues even more so. Dr. Vornberg is the epitome of servant leadership and his wife, Caroline, is also an exemplary educator, colleague, and friend.

Dr. Rhonda Lucich, Justin Smith, Georgia Holt, Judith Niemann Black, Gene Theriac, Cindy Frost Burns, Jimmy Sikes, and Dr. Justin Terry contributed their expertise and vision of education as our shadowbox voices from the field. These incredible educators have made a distinct mark on our profession in their professional practice and we greatly appreciate the time they took to share their reflections with us to augment the book.

Educators are not good marketers and we had the help of great friend Steve Weir to help us with the final title and cover design, which we lamented over for weeks. A cover and title are so important to a browser purchasing your book and Steve and his team at Lead Concepts Inc. provided many ideas and such deliberate guidance for us to figure it out. Thank you, Steve!

There are schools we have worked with and worked in that have provided so much depth, verification, and codification to our work. Terry Lapic, Justin Terry, Judy Webber, Dr. Leslie Feinglas, Julie Haba, Jon Peters, Tami Nauyokas, Rick Nolla, Michelle Fowler Hooper, Sharon Hill, Steve Green, Farrah Gomez, Travis Benintendo, Donna Gallegos, and the many teachers that have allowed us into their classrooms to work with them and their students—we thank you. You are courageous educators that are demonstrative of the educators we have dedicated this book.

Our colleagues and staffs, past and present, have provided many deeds that influenced our work over the years and ultimately this book. Dr. Julie Peterson Combs and Dr. Casey Graham Brown continue to inspire and challenge us. Robert Henson, Debbie Allen, Camille Malone, Carol Beene, and Jan Braswell always provided whatever help or assistance was needed even when we didn't know it was needed. Dr. Nicole Johnson, Dr. John L. Garcia, Dr. Ann Carns, and Dr. Mike Carns have influenced our work in many lasting ways.

We both have a powerful circle of close friends, more so like family, that affect our thinking, our humor, and ultimately our disposition for teaching and sharing with others. When you write about changing things as profoundly as our volume dictates, it's important to keep our expectations real and our vision centered. Rob Auman, Dr. Matthew Ingraham, Dr. Russell Marshall, Keith Owen, Worth Ross, Debbie Sanderson and David Rogers do that for us and their love, care, and friendships are invaluable and unconditional. Everyone needs friends and we are both blessed to have perhaps more than we deserve, both in quality and quantity.

Finally, this book was almost a year late in its completion (largely due to Timothy) that was as a result of a wonderful epiphany during what was the final months of the first draft. Sometimes people come into our lives and we sometimes never totally understand why but are forever changed. As Timothy contemplated the very context for this book he was first touched by a soon-to-be college graduate that was both the benefactor and a casualty of a public education in the United States. His story is of largely being one of those silent consumers of our system, little resistance throughout his schooling but instead simply a willing consumer of what we offered each day. He trusted us, always did what we asked of him, and ultimately graduated. Then he put himself through a public university. It all sounds like a benefactor of the system until you see the debt he had to accumulate just to live a meager existence in school, working twenty-five to thirty hours a week at a bank that believed in him but saddled with an ever-growing school debt that would choke a seasoned and established adult, much less a young adult setting out in life. Derek Adam is both an amazing and inspiring guy. While this book doesn't reach into the issues and problems of postsecondary education, those problems clearly will have to be addressed in our total system's return to greatness. We need an educated workforce but to burden them with such huge debt is simply not sustainable. Derek's love, attitude, optimism, compassion, and techno-savviness reinvigorated and changed Timothy's field of vision for that return to greatness and it's obviously repeated throughout the rewrite of this volume. To be sure, education today has changed greatly since the days the authors were in school and, for at least one of us, to see the current system through Derek's lens was totally enlightening and made a substantial difference in the final book. I am very proud of you, Derek, and deeply appreciate and love the many lessons you have taught me for education and for life.

To all of you, we give our deepest thanks!

Introduction

Harnessing the Dynamics of Public Education: Preparing for a Return to Greatness

There is an infection spreading in the American public school. It is a dangerous, brain-deadening virus that threatens to corrode the minds of all who inhabit our schools and to eventually tear down the schools themselves. It is a very complex virus continuously mutating and manifesting itself in many forms. It is highly resistant to treatment. Moreover, what makes this virus especially dangerous is that it often masks itself as a cure. This disease is an ancient one cultivated long ago that initially fostered a healthy treatment for many of society's ills.

This culture (pun intended) has festered and turned putrid, yet we continue to willfully spread it and wonder aloud why we are ill. The disease is standardization and our public schools need a cure that counters this virus and eradicates it. For that cure to truly take effect, public schools in the United States must change! Many band-aids, remedies, and elixirs (i.e., programs, reforms, and initiatives) have been applied over the years, but they have only treated the symptom, or worse, served as placebos—public education has remained unchanged at its core.

It is irrelevant whether or not we desire this change or believe in its necessity. The cold, hard fact is that public schools must adapt or die. There is no middle ground. The future survival of public education in America depends upon our coming to grips with this reality. No more denial. No more swallowing the disease and calling it the cure. It is time to begin an aggressive treatment program.

American democracy has served as a model for the world. This democracy was built, in no small part, via its public education system. Our nation was founded on principles born of and contingent upon free, public education for all citizens. Indeed, Thomas Jefferson emphasized how vital education would be to building a healthy democracy.

However, since the Soviet launch of Sputnik in 1957, public education in the modern era has been increasingly blamed for America's failures—perceived and real—and thus targeted for reforms to right the perceived wrongs. The ante was raised in 1983 with the publication of *A Nation at Risk: The Imperative for Educational Reform* (1983) by the National Commission on Excellence in Education. The reform movement expanded, and this time it took on a more hardened and negative tone toward public education. Indeed, since that report, "hundreds, if not thousands of books and articles have been written, and millions if not billions of dollars have been spent [on education reform]" (Jones, 2013, p. 1).

So what has all this time, money, effort, and handwringing over the last fifty years produced? In schools today do we see an innovative and modern educational system that meets the demands of America's students in the twenty-first century and prepares them for the challenges of tomorrow? No, sadly the more things have changed, the more they have stayed the same. And while we have seen dramatic shifts in the structure of business, medicine, and communications since that launch of Sputnik almost sixty years ago, our public education system still mirrors the one-room schoolhouse romanticized in *Little House on the Prairie*.

One could argue that with all the rapid changes in the world, it is nice to have some constancy and stability with our educational system. That would be true if our system was working—unfortunately it is not. Our mission, however, remains the same. Thus, to return our public education system to its once lofty status in the world, we must shatter tradition to maintain continuity with the past. The one-room schoolhouse served America well during its agrarian era. Indeed, this icon is a powerful symbol of our democratic roots in public education. It also makes for cute crafts and decorations, but it should not form the basis for how we actually structure our twenty-first-century schools.

Despite the decades of rhetoric and alleged reform and restructuring:

> Most would agree that little has substantially changed in the average public school classroom. The twenty-first-century school is merely a row or collection of one-room schoolhouses conveniently joined together under one roof yet maintaining the ideals, mission, models, and methods of the agrarian time period in which it was created. (Jones, 2013, p. 1–2)

When the classroom teacher closes the door, our students are shut off from the rest of the world; closed off from reality and thrust into an artificially conscripted dictatorship where knowledge is broken down into ever-smaller parts. Where is the whole? Where is the connection to the world at large and to the student's life in particular?

It is no wonder why students feel disconnected in such a scenario. As Dan Haesler (2013) pointed out, where else in the world are you forced to only be with people your own age, forced to be engaged on a specific topic at a set time (and if you do get engaged, you have to disengage when we tell you), and forced to urinate at the same time as everyone else?

Because our system has clung to an outdated paradigm at its core, over the last five decades we have chosen window dressing and feel-good policy-making over transformative growth. One thing has changed dramatically, however: The rhetoric has shifted and the stakes have risen. Reform and restructuring have given way to alternatives and choice.

The choice movement which began with allowing choices among public schools has now shifted to allowing a choice of any school option with the use of vouchers. Vouchers, theoretically, would be the ultimate choice. This option would provide parents with a voucher equivalent to the dollar amount the state spends per pupil and would allow those parents to spend it on any school to which his or her child is admitted. Voucher proponents and some political think tanks tout this concept by telling parents that with the voucher they can put their child in the best schools available without paying private school tuition. We call this the Everyone Can Go to Harvard Theory (Jones, 2013, p. 11), a notion we believe is utter nonsense in actual practice.

Reflecting on the years since *A Nation at Risk*, the obvious question seems to be, has public education sufficiently improved? If the answer were yes, would we even find ourselves in a discussion about vouchers? Has our nation reached the point where we are willing to explore the destruction of public education in America as we know it only to replace it with a private, free-market yet publicly funded system? It seems that we are. Thus, it begs the question, is this exploration based upon legitimate and scientific concern or is it driven by other factors? Is education policy based upon sound education theory and practice or is it driven by political whimsy and special interests?

For us, it seems that both are not possible. America either builds and funds a world-class public education system that achieves the critical goals and objectives of an informed democratic society, or it decides the achievement of those goals and objectives are better left to the free-market system. We believe it must be one or the other, because we do not believe the American economy can afford to do both. Such an attempt would result in two underfunded systems that would never reach world-class status and thus foster mediocrity at best.

Is this to say we believe we should continue the model of reform and restructure? To be sure, we do not! "We come to bury Caesar, not to praise him." However, do we embrace the voucher movement that ultimately would abandon the 150-year-old mission of public schools? We absolutely do not! So what is the answer? How does America return to the status of intellectual excellence it once enjoyed in the world? What is the path that returns American public education to greatness?

In defining what the path is, it can help to define what it is not. We do not believe the path for the return to greatness for public education is traveled via a for-profit or free-market solution. We do not believe this path to be either cost effective or performance effective and, despite the assertions of the privatization advocates, there is little evidence to contradict us. Consequently, we embrace drivers that will ensure a path to greatness in public education that include:

> Driver 1—A school that demonstrates a respect for and understanding of what made public schools great and the ability to build upon what worked and replace what either did not or is now obsolete.
> Driver 2—A school that reflects a deep understanding and celebration of how America has changed in complexity, demographics, economics, and social structures.
> Driver 3—A school that embraces, engages, responds, and reacts to criticism and attacks, both political and social, by the various stakeholders of the school.
> Driver 4—A school that encourages and self-directs a comprehensive system of accountability and improvement.
> Driver 5—A school that has overcome the rigid pedagogical paralysis that overwhelms most schools today and instead is indicative of ongoing advanced pedagogical development of teachers and administrators that recognizes the emerging and game-changing advances in the neurosciences.
> Driver 6—A school that demands highly skilled, innovative, and authentic leadership that recognizes the complex nature of teaching and learning.
> Driver 7—A school that embraces and ensures physical, emotional, and intellectual safety.

Since the publication of *A Nation at Risk*, the role of education in the global economy is more vital now than ever before. Equally true is the premise that education can and should come in multiple forms and be dependent more upon achievement and performance than on outdated and constrictive notions of tradition. Again, we must shatter tradition to maintain continuity with the past.

This book will delve into many of the preconceived notions and paradigms that must be shattered. A mere paradigm shift is not enough. The term *shift* is still too mechanistic to work in our systemic world. We need to create a paradigm blend akin to Peter Senge's (2006) term *metanoia*.

This paradigm blend will permeate education at all levels. It will be challenging and force us to rethink and reevaluate many traditions we take for granted. For example, as Sir Ken Robinson (2009) illustrated, we have learned through advances in neuroscience and memory that our common practice of teaching to the masses (the larger group) is neither efficient nor ultimately effective. Learning is both an individual process and an innately social one as well. Schools, like society, should be too! Sir Robinson suggests:

> Given the challenges we face, education doesn't need to be reformed—it needs to be transformed. The key to this transformation is not to standardize education, but to personalize it, to build achievement on discovering the individual talents of each child, to put students in an environment where they want to learn and where they can naturally discover their true passions. (p. 238)

This paradigm blend won't be an easy task. There are many moving parts to American public education. For starters, we have fifty states with multiple school organizations and systems both publicly and privately funded and regulated. Within those systems, there are elementary and secondary philosophies, and within individual schools, there are grade levels and differing needs of learners. Our vision for greatness in public schools is not to prescribe a single solution or ascribe to a single system. We believe this would not only be impossible, but would miss out on great possibility in human potential development.

Instead, we proffer a set of ideas that can be embraced in any school organization or system, either public or private. To effect this change, leaders must do just that—lead, and lead by example. Our leaders will need to create the structure, the container, within which learning and growth are fostered. We need our leaders to create a holistic accountability system that promotes this growth and success. Not one that fosters a blame game; yielding manipulation and spin control rather than actual education. Decisions must be grounded in sound theory and science, not special interests groups.

Educators should have a greater say in the school calendar than the tourism industry for example. This will take courage. The Greatest Generation overcame the Great Depression and two world wars. The twentieth century was defined by industrialization, large-scale war, and major strides in technology. The twenty-first century may well be defined by how we transform education (or don't).

Our greatest resource on this planet is the human resource, the human mind. In our public schools that resource is our teachers, staff, and students. How we foster and nurture this resource will greatly affect how we allocate, develop, and preserve the other resources our planet has to offer. Twenty-first century needs are big—population, climate change, energy, water, food, and peace/stability pose big challenges. Will America's public education system generate leaders and thinkers to solve these problems or stay mired in an antiquated system?

Businesses don't sell products anymore. They sell solutions. Our education system needs to be in the business of creating solutions. We must break away from the shackles of the factory-model, product-oriented concept of education. Education is a process, not a product. Standardization is great for producing cars on an assembly line. It is not great for producing critically thinking, contributing citizens in a democracy.

As Caine (2013) points out, getting there from here will take time and concerted effort. By nature, our species does not embrace rapid change. Indeed, it has been said that it takes one hundred years to change a culture. As John Dewey put it, "Man is not logical and his intellectual history is a record of mental reserves and compromises. He hangs on to what he can in his old beliefs even when he is compelled to surrender their logical basis" (Gouinlock, 1994, p. 70). Public education will need to transcend this aspect of human nature. It will need to transcend fear. While this is not instinctive, it is possible. Moreover it is paramount. Technology is changing the world at an exponential rate. It is imperative our education system at least keep pace.

Yes, our solution for greatness is as effective in a private or charter school as it would be in a public one. However, we strongly believe that a world-class public education system is the most cost effective, performance effective for all students and thus the only ultimate solution for an informed electorate in a democratic society. In short, our solution reflects the belief that parents' best choice for preparing their child to be successful in a changing global economy is with a high-quality public education. We need education of the people, by the people, and for the people.

References

Caine, G. (2013, summer). Education cannot get where it wants to go because it cannot see where it needs to go: Seeing "learning" in a new light. *School Leadership Review, 8*(2), 17–34.

Gouinlock, J. (1994). *The moral writings of John Dewey.* Amherst, NY: Prometheus Books.

Haesler, D. (2013). 3 Rules that only apply in schools. Retrieved from http://danhaesler.com/doodlesbydan/#jp-carousel-3103

Jones, T. B. (2013). *Education for the human brain: A road map to natural learning in schools.* Lanham, MD: Rowman and Littlefield.

National Commission on Excellence in Education. (1983). *A nation at risk: The imperative for educational reform.* Washington, DC: Author.

Robinson, K. (2009). *The element: How finding your passion changes everything.* New York: Penguin Books.

Senge, P. (2006). *The fifth discipline: The art and practice of the learning organization.* New York: Doubleday.

1
Building a Naturally Great School

> Every experienced physician knows that attempting to overcome disease by trying to eradicate the pathogen head-on is generally a losing battle. Battles of will with viruses, bacteria, and malignant cells are generally weary and ineffective at best. Even with enormous medicinal or mechanical power at hand, the physician will always have more success if he or she can promote the organism's own natural capacity to win and natural will to survive. Most parents, managers, and mentors (teachers, therapists, and consultants) have not learned this lesson, however. They still believe that they can teach, motivate, and inculcate values in their charges simply by exerting enough will, without due regard for the natural forces that work against such well-meaning efforts, but which, as with the sailor and the physician, can be harnessed to the leader's helm.
>
> —Edwin H. Friedman, *A Failure of Nerve*

True story: a principal in Texas once stated, "Our school would be great if it weren't for the kids." This statement, obviously born of frustration, is not only disconcerting, ironic, and comical, it really gets to the heart of the matter, to the core of education. This is where it all begins and where it should all end as well: with the student. Yet, how often is that the case? For all the complications and controversies surrounding education, isn't it really just a simple thing? Learning is innate; it is natural. Humans are hardwired to learn; indeed, all animals are wired that way. Why then has education become something so controversial, convoluted, and contentious? This chapter begins that exploration by examining where public education has been, where it is going, what the overall objective is, and what the best way to achieve a naturally great school is.

Using the scientific lens of living systems, we start with the individual and expand outward ripple by ripple. Education is a process. It is a relationship. It is a relationship between relationships: teacher to student, student to teacher, student to student, student to knowledge, and knowledge to knowledge. Learning is about connection—human connection and knowledge connection. Learning doesn't happen in a vacuum; it happens in a context. This is a vital supposition because where we begin decides where we will go. If we approach schooling from a mechanistic, product-oriented philosophy, then we end up where we are.

But if we approach schooling from a systems perspective, rooted in the new scientific understanding of how the brain learns and human society functions, then it can no longer be business as usual; we must move in new directions. If education is simply the transmission of knowledge—of remembering facts and listening to experts—then we can follow our path in the structure of this transmission or even choose the banal online curriculums many for-profits are touting. But, if we view learning through the lens of the human brain—through growth, maturation, and renewal—then we must alter our course in favor of a more complex, multifaceted route.

This book will take you on this route: examining the research, raising questions, offering solutions, and encouraging educators and community members to transform the educational system by harnessing the power of natural learning. Simply by reading this text, you are taking that first step. For the act of reading is not passive. As American author Kurt Vonnegut describes it, "It's like arriving at a concert hall and being handed a violin, and you're expected to play. That's what we expect readers to do, perform themselves, because they're half of the performance."

We begin this journey by building upon the strengths of our educational system. This book will also serve as a springboard for you, the reader. We will not try to answer everything; this is not a prescription. Rather our goal is to provoke and inspire you into problem solving. Our greatest national resource is our human resource. Tapping into that and into the American spirit of pioneering and ingenuity will be the best path to academic excellence in America.

To that end, we stipulate six premises:

1. Public schools are a cornerstone of American democracy and the American dream. Public schools are a critical component of the American economy and provide the best choice for a quality education. The American public will be best served in investing in the restructuring of public schools instead of the creation of alternative educational options.
2. Making schools better for all learners does not mean fixing what we have; rather it means reconceptualizing what we do in schools and how we do it. Schools and school leaders need to reexamine age-old issues, structures, models, and instructional and curricular challenges with a different perceptual orientation and frame of reference.
3. Schools that will be significantly better will not only be different from what is regarded as the traditional school, but they will also be wholly unique. There is no panacea or cookie cutter for great schools other than strong leaders and a focused purpose. These schools will be different: organizationally poised to learn and grow, particularly pedagogically, because of advances in brain research, human potential, computer technologies and a revitalized focus on constant and continuous betterment.
4. School improvement and success is not measured by performance on standardized minimum skills tests but rather in overtly striving to meet the individual potential of learners.

5. Professional educators have an ethical obligation to document and share their experiences, knowledge, and innovations with the educational profession and academia.
6. The principal is not the only key leader in making schools better. In fact, a number of different school leaders can fundamentally change learning and help teachers transform learning in their classroom using the latest practices and pedagogy (Jones, 2013, pp. 2–3).

The Strength of Letting Go

Harnessing the dynamics of change and human potential will require a major mind shift in education. This shift has already occurred in several other fields and therefore it can be done. It isn't easy, however, and requires letting go of old ways of thinking—like Linus giving up his security blanket—and it is essential. It is also paradoxical in nature: to create lasting and effective change in education, we must give up control. We must let go of a fixed mindset and of a need to control everything.

Education leaders must be like the basketball coaches who design effective plays, yet allow their players to utilize their talents and decision-making skills within that framework. We will be better served to control what is important and then allow the natural renewal process to take place within those parameters. This is a strength-based approach. The focus is to build upon the strengths of what is already working.

Many reformers and critics want to tear everything down and build from scratch. The erase-and-replace mentality is very inefficient and expensive, and is born out of a problem-saturated perspective. These naysayers are hyper-focusing on the 10 percent of things that need improvement and ignoring the 90 percent of things that are working. This mentality, strongly rooted in the mechanistic, product-oriented perspective, actually serves to exacerbate the problem.

Viewing education through this problem-saturated lens has led to greater and greater control. This is a very natural reaction. If individuals see that something isn't working (by their standard) then they move in to fix it. And when it continues to not live up to their expectations, they work harder and harder to fix it. In a mechanical sense, for example, fixing an automotive engine, this approach works.

But for the modern educational system, the irony of what has happened is that the greater control exerted, the greater the reigns have been tightened, the worse the problem has become, not better. This fixed mindset has led to a system wherein thoroughbred horses have been diminished into pack mules.

Pack Mules and Thoroughbreds

The tightening of the reigns as we know it began in the 1950s when the Soviet Union launched the Sputnik satellite into space. With our rivals being the first to launch a satellite into space, America's perceived failure was pinned directly on the shoulders of its public school system. Thus began the fashionable practice of using public education as the national whipping boy, the sacrificial lamb whose slaughter would appease the gods of American capitalism and military prowess. This practice has grown ever worse. For now it isn't just the system that is being attacked and blamed, but the teachers themselves (e.g., the cover story of *Time* magazine, Edwards, 2014).

But educators aren't evildoers bent on undermining the American dream, nor are they incompetent slackers. Quite the opposite. The majority of teachers enter the profession with a burning desire to make a difference in children's lives. It is precisely this strength that needs to be harnessed. Our teachers desire to be thoroughbreds and we need to unleash this energy and direct it in a positive manner. Instead, we burden these racehorses, weighing them down and sucking their vitality so that they either leave or they are forced to trod along at a slow, narrow pace. A similar dynamic happens with our students as well.

Learning Is Unstoppable

Humans learn, period. What they learn, when they learn, and how they learn are factors that our educational system seeks to control. Even the students whose teachers lament are not learning a thing in their class are still learning something. They just are not learning what the teacher wants them to learn (or at the desired pace or in the proscribed manner).

If learning is a given for humans (and all animals), what then is its purpose? There are, arguably, two instinctual purposes for education: survival and curiosity. The first purpose is rooted in a primal, instinctive need. The second purpose is rooted in more abstract thought and the brain's natural instinct to ask "why?" Joldersma (2011) used the term *conatus* to describe this first purpose and humankind's striving to live.

This striving is the primordial need for understanding. Certain knowledge must be passed on to one's offspring to help them survive. As Christian (2011) illustrated, a species' survival depends on knowledge that is passed down or learned through experience. This is true whether we are speaking of a lion cub learning to hunt or a human learning to swim or studying engineering—knowledge and know-how mean survival.

While this conatus of learning is evident in all animals, the second purpose appears to be unique to humans. This yearning for a more abstract understanding of "why" we live in addition to the basic understanding of "how" to live is not new, it predates even the ancient philosophers. It seems that since the dawn of humankind, people have looked for ways to explain the unexplainable.

Every culture has a creation myth. Every culture has found ways to explain the seasons, dramatic changes in the weather, and other aspects of nature and reality. While the first purpose is a more mundane and preliminary goal: survival—both physical and social; the second purpose is more abstract and deals with facilitating a deeper understanding.

These two purposes for learning seem to be inherent in human education. The ancient Greek philosopher Plato serves as an example of an early advocate for both purposes of education. For example, his utopian republic was based on a survival of the fittest model (with survival as a primary force for education), Plato described what could be called a higher purpose of education: "The ultimate end of all education is insight into the harmonious order (cosmos) of the whole world" (Cornford, 1941, p. 88).

These two aims seem to be successive in nature and are likely akin to Maslow's hierarchy of needs. Before teaching a pupil the "understanding of the cosmos," it would behoove the teacher to educate the pupil in the ways of physical and social survival. A person is less likely to be interested in the nature of the universe when he or she is unemployed and starving. The questions for the present educator are these: What purposes (if any) are we fulfilling with our present system? Are we meeting the survival needs of our students? And, are we encouraging students to gain that ultimate understanding? How does public education balance these two purposes? To help answer these questions we start with the educators.

The Educators

Outside of the individual learner, few people, if any, would argue any dependent variable in education more critical than the professional educator. As it is often said, teachers are where the rubber meets the road. Indeed, there is a plethora of research that demonstrates the important role the individual teacher plays in student success.

Yet, what is the definition of the teacher's role in modern education? How does the individual educator master such a vital position given all the demands that must be balanced? How much autonomy and decision-making power do the people in these vital roles possess? How much should they possess?

Once upon a time, *educator* meant the classroom teacher or even the schoolmarm. A school might comprise a single teacher or perhaps a few classroom teachers and a building principal who served essentially as a facilities manager. Today the term includes a cadre of highly trained professionals delivering services from assessment, diagnostics, counseling, and social work

Voices from the Field

My grandparents were hardworking farmers as were their parents. In a one-room schoolhouse, boys went to school through the eighth grade; girls through the fifth. The necessity of a basic education was clear, and in those few years, they learned what they needed to know. Reading and math were about the Sears catalog, managing bank loans, ordering seed, following sewing patterns, canning enough vegetables to last through the winter, selling cotton and peanuts at a profit, writing letters to loved ones. Reading and math mattered, and teachers understood the needs of their students.

There were no air conditioners, no libraries, no computers, no cafeterias, no supplies beyond pencil and paper, and, yet, though quite substandard compared to today's campuses, schools held an esteemed place at the community's center. The ability to apply what had been learned was the full measure of a successful education. Schools served their purpose well. They were great.

Lest you think this is one of those "walked three miles in the snow to get to school" stories with the theme song from Little House on the Prairie playing softly in the background, let's consider it a jumping off point. What else was missing? There were no standardized tests, no Campus Improvement Teams, no written curricula, no expectation that every child be college ready, no school performance ratings, no unfunded mandates, no vouchers, no teacher rating system, no cry for national standards, no politicians campaigning based on their party-written educational plaforms. Although each of these was proposed as a mechanism for returning our schools to glory, from my perspective, we were never lost.

I would contend that the single most important factor in a child's education—regardless whether it has taken place in a one-room schoolhouse or beautiful, modern structure—has always been, and continues to be, what happens within those four classroom walls, between the teacher and the student. No technology, curriculum, or test will make nearly such a difference. Children have always known when a teacher genuinely cared about them and their learning.

That relationship is key. I have witnessed it over and over again. When a new student enrolled, a fifth grade boy who had already been retained twice and was still unable to write both his first and last name correctly, his teacher scooped him up and refused to let him continue

> *to fail. She loved him. He loved her. She performed at the superhuman level. He gave her all he had. She tutored him and his younger brother daily. She went to his ballgames. She met with his mother to show her how to assist with home practice. She sprinkled glitter over him while he worked. At the end of the year, we all cried when it was time for him to graduate from elementary school. He was performing almost on level.*
>
> *We now know so much more about the brain and learning; we have magnificent resources available; we have made great strides to ensure that education is available for all. With such tremendous access in this informational and technological age, the nightly news still reports that our schools are failing. Elected officials routinely submit that we are not doing as well as we should, or as well as schools in other countries. My position is that our schools are not broken;* **the lens through which they are looking is broken.** *It's not about the performance of schools in other countries. It never has been. Great teachers make great schools, and every parent who has watched their child's growth while in such a classroom, knows it. Invest in those teachers and everything else will fall into place.*
>
> —Rhonda Lucich,
> Garland Independent School District
> Garland, Texas

to school leadership, grant writing, and data disaggregation and analysis. There is no question that over time professional educators have become vaster as needs of students and communities have dictated it.

Building upon the strengths of educators, requires a reflection on past success. As we look back, we find that several of the needs mentioned previously still existed, however, the available human resources were limited to the teacher (and often the community's sole teacher). While it may seem to be a great expectation and responsibility for the early day schoolmarm, the fact is that teachers had enormous autonomy. Because of that autonomy, they understood that they lived on a daily basis for the needs and progress of the students.

Teacher autonomy did not just exist in the classroom. A student that the teacher would have in first grade would be with that teacher until that student finished school. Consequently, if the student had trouble with one reading task or learning another math skill, the teacher directed his or her own development to find other ways to teach the skill or other strategies to reach that child. Although often trial-by-fire, professional development for the pedagogy of the teacher became immediately relevant and self-directed because not figuring out how to effectively teach that student would be the problem that kept on giving year after year.

As schools became larger and more specialized, the autonomy of the teacher was diminished. To be sure, today's classroom teacher enjoys a great deal of autonomy, but most of that autonomy is limited to how learning is to occur for an increasingly large group of students simultaneously. The teacher is no longer autonomous in what is to be taught, to what extent it will be mastered, what goals are reasonable for the students, how the school day will be structured, how long or when the school day will occur, or what resources will be utilized.

Teachers today control far less from when we were great (whether one hundred years ago or twenty-five years ago) and the truth is that that pattern has continued over a large span of time. As times changed and the world got more complicated, teachers had to become more specialized, which required more people in the educational equation. The more people involved in the education of the child, the less autonomy any one teacher has with that child.

Specialization is not necessarily bad, but as we learn from what made us great, we have to recognize that the generalist approach yielded an educator more attune to the needs of the student and because of simplicity was much more able to make immediate changes or adjustments to the ebb and flow of that child's education. This would certainly foster a perception of an educator more in touch with individual needs of the learner than perhaps our system today.

The School

As educators have become more specialized and comprehensive, the school itself had to change to accommodate this. At the beginning of our agrarian school system, the school itself was very simple. In fact, it was not unusual for the learning of the community to be done outside or in a building used for other purposes.

There were many children in the first fifty years or so of American schools that learned in the same place as the community worshipped. The teacher shared the same space with the pastor. As communities grew, so did the school and over time went from a one-room school to a variety of sizes, up to thousands of students and hundreds of educators with the teacher being just one type.

Technology has perhaps been the most significant influence on the change in the physical school building itself. Classrooms were designed with just a couple of electrical outlets. The clock, the film projector, and maybe an overhead projector were all you needed to utilize the latest technology for learning. Today, those classrooms have been retrofitted to utilize all types of technology centered on computers, tablets, and connectivity. Consequently, the school today is more complex and requires highly technical skills to maintain technology and information systems.

As schools have become more complex, they also continue to become larger. A modern urban or suburban high school, for example, might house three or four thousand students and employ three to four hundred teachers and other professional educators. While clearly no longer a one-room schoolhouse, some have argued that the large school is not much more than a string or row of one-room school houses (Jones, 2013) conveniently organized to accommodate a growing community.

The complexity of the profession as earlier discussed has resulted in more people that are generally more specialized and thus require more space in which to work. Add the impact of technology in the classroom and student needs too, and it's no surprise that schools continue to get larger. It is obvious that the size of the school has increased as a result of more students and more educational professionals providing services. However, have the technological requirements of the modern educator (particularly the classroom teacher) kept up with the technological advancements of the school itself? Has modern pedagogy kept pace with technological advances and greater connectivity?

The greatest hope for our public schools is to help our educators harness their own potential and the natural learning potential within each individual learner. Our students have the greatest potential to create the lasting change we seek in our educational system and our nation as a whole. Students quite literally are the future. The students are not merely a *product* of our schools, rather they are an integral asset.

The old model of education has been built upon a system that does something to students. We take a blob of clay and mold it into what we want, regardless of what type of clay it is or what the clay wants for itself. This new model focuses on helping the clay shape itself and building upon the inherent strengths within the clay. There is much talk of student-centered and personalized learning, but what does that mean in modern education? In fact, under our agrarian system, our schools were already much more student-centered and personalized.

It is when we adopted the factory model for education during the first half of the twentieth century that we moved into the standardized model we still see today. The challenge now is to bring back the strengths of the early American education system and integrate them into a more complex system. The key paradox for our return to greatness is to find simplicity within complexity.

The System

The truth is, education has enjoyed many decades of praise and esteem from the tax-paying public. Public educators are almost always included in top-ten lists of most respected professions or professionals. Even more interesting is that even with all the attacks on public education, school teachers still rank very high in most respected professions.

The annual Phi Delta Kappa study consistently documents that even people with concerns for public education still rank their teachers or their children's teachers high in esteem, competence, and respect. Consequently, it would be silly in looking forward to not understand this phenomenon and build upon that very strong foundation.

It is no surprise that as education has changed, the educational enterprise has changed as well. When education in America began, schools were almost completely locally controlled. A local community decided if and when to have school, who would teach and where schooling would occur.

Consequently, a school in one community could and did appear very different than a school in another community. The community decided what curriculum would be taught and hired someone that would determine how the curriculum would be taught and to what extent it would have to be learned. Not only was the what, how, and to what extent locally controlled, the funding of the enterprise was also decided by local decisions.

It is as American as apple pie for money to pay for specific things to be attached to regulations, conditions, or strings. Public education in the United States is not only evidence of that, it is most likely one of the most affected examples. Our founding fathers acknowledged early on that a democracy would require an informed electorate.

The U.S. Constitution does not specifically address public education, and so through the Reserved Powers Clause (Tenth Amendment) the responsibility for an electorate capable of being informed fell upon the state governments. Over time, every state in the union developed compulsory attendance laws and a system of public education for the state. Consequently, the state began paying some or all of the cost of that education system and it grew in numbers and complexity as time went on, populations grew, and needs changed.

As costs have shifted from the local community for education, so has the control of the school with a constant battle continuing between the state and the local school. Additionally, in the 1960s, the federal government decided to enter the school enterprise and with it another set of strings and regulations tied to another level of funding. All of this has fostered an educational system with many levels, funding sources, regulations, and laws that are far removed from the local community school that the system had originated.

Hence, the constituencies and stakeholders of the typical public school system are vast, multileveled, and complicating.

When we were great, school systems were simpler to access and less complicating to understand and thus easier to adapt and evolve in a changing world.

Springboard to Greatness

Somewhere along the way, modern American education has lost sight of the innate drive to learn. A look back at American educational history will yield elements of greatness and innovation. It will also yield elements of shame, for while it profited many, it also neglected, rejected, and exploited many. From a strength-based approach, our new container model for education builds upon the greatness inherent within the American educational ideal and integrates it with the modern challenges and opportunities.

America's greatest resource is its human resource. Public education is the best way to harness the greatness of its people and unleash their potential. The challenge we face is taking the elements of greatness from the old model and implementing it at a much larger scale and in the modern context. Public education can, and must, meet the demands of the two basic purposes for education: survival and understanding. The educators, the school, and the system will need a shift of mind and a paradigm blend to accomplish this (Barrett, 2013).

Learning is about connection. In our return to greatness, the individual learner needs to connect to his or her local community and to the broader global community. The survival goal for public education is to develop global, digital citizens prepared for the modern workforce and instilled with the yearning for greater understanding.

References

Barrett, D. C. (summer, 2013). Holistic, ethical leadership for the 21st century. *School Leadership Review, 8*(2), 41–51.

Christian, J. L. (2011). *Philosophy: An introduction to the art of wondering.* 11th edition, Boston: Wadsworth.

Cornford, F. M. (1941). *The republic of Plato*. New York: Oxford University Press.

Edwards, H. S. (2014, October 30). The war on teacher tenure. *Time*. Retrieved from http://time.com/3533556/the-war-on-teacher-tenure/

Joldersma, C. W. (2011). Education: Understanding, ethics, and the call of justice. *Studies in Philosophy and Education, 30*, 441–47. DOI 10.007/s11217-011-9246-7.

Jones, T. B. (2013). *Education for the human brain: A roadmap to natural learning in schools*. Lanham, MD: Rowman and Littlefield.

2
Fostering a New Mindset for the Future

> Where you come from is gone, where you thought you were going to never was there.
>
> —Flannery O'Connor

Does the phrase, "Kodak moment" ring a bell? For more than one hundred years Eastman Kodak monopolized the American camera and film marketplace—in 1976 it controlled 90 percent of film sales and 85 percent of camera sales. Moreover, Kodak was regularly rated as one of the world's five most valuable brands.

Founded in 1880 by George Eastman, the company was known as a pioneer and innovator in film and photography. For over a century the company and its influence grew with little rival. In the late 1980s, the company had over 145,000 employees worldwide. Kodak's revenues continued to climb, peaking at nearly $16 billion in 1996 with its profits topping out at $2.5 billion in 1999.

Flash forward to 2012, and the 132-year-old international giant had shrunk to a company with less than 15,000 and was filing for bankruptcy. Eastman Kodak is a shell of the global, corporate power it once was. So what happened? In a nutshell, Kodak's main product, film, became obsolete with new technology. Due to arrogance and a culture of complacency, the company didn't adapt and it went under.

The company is now reemerging as a smaller, leaner company; a company that is fighting for its share of a crowded industry. It is now trying to return to greatness, but it is, perhaps, too late (*The Economist*, 2012; McCammon, 2013; Rao, 2014).

Public education faces its own possible Kodak moment. Similar to the once dominant company, the world is a very different place from the time of the founding of America's educational system. Likewise, our large institution has a monopoly, but it is losing marketshare and facing a very different future. The question is thus, will American public education go the way of the dinosaurs or will it adapt and change to meet the demands of the twenty-first century?

This chapter explores this question and posits three answers: (1) the American public school is not a dead man walking, (2) to survive and thrive, public schools must shatter tradition to maintain continuity with the past, and (3) a container model will allow for the proper balance of structure and creativity in our school system.

Dead Man Walking

Public education in America is not dead yet, but its survival is being propped up. While there are many parallels with the story of Kodak, there is one major difference: Kodak didn't have an automatic customer base. Public schools benefit from this automatic customer base with little to no competition. In fact, if you don't use our service, we will take you to court. Yet, even with this mandated customer base, we are still gradually losing marketshare and, more important, we are losing public confidence and trust.

We are also being stripped of funding. Public education is at a crossroads of survival. This book overall, and this chapter in particular, is not intended to be a harbinger of doom and gloom; quite the contrary, we see many signs of hope. However, it is time for a wake-up call, a time for true change. Mere window dressing or a rearranging of furniture on the deck of the *Titanic* will not suffice. Public education will need to become more nimble and more agile to compete in an ever-changing global market with increased competition.

At the most basic level, the needs of students are the same now as they were at the formation of our school system. The manner in which we meet those needs, however, has changed dramatically and it will continue to change. Moreover, the knowledge and skills necessary for a productive citizenry have radically shifted. Our current system is not designed for this. We must adapt or die.

Education is not a zero-sum game, but we are competing for our survival. We are not only competing for students and resources, but also for the attention of the students we have. There are far more enticing alternatives to employ their attention and technology magnifies those distractions—just think of the ubiquitous cell phone and how it has incrementally infiltrated our classrooms and our lives over the last fifteen years.

Now think about other new technologies being developed like Google Glass and how they will infiltrate our classrooms. How will we compete in this realm? The answer lies in shifting our focus. It can't be shifted to something gimmicky or flashy; we must stay rooted in solid pedagogy, but we need to adapt our approach or die a slow death.

This book is a defense of public education, but, as you've likely gleaned, it is not a defense of the current system. We recognize the need for dramatic changes. We advocate for changes that fit with the true nature of reality grounded in science and the new findings from research in brain-compatible learning, organizational growth, and self-renewal. Our current system is archaic, but there are many people who profit from it and many people within it who are entrenched in these ways and unwilling to change.

To paraphrase Spencer Johnson (1998), they don't want their cheese moved. But change is inevitable, and as Paul D. Houston, former executive director for the American Association of School Superintendents (AASA) wrote, "We seek change when the status quo isn't what we want. But it doesn't matter. The fact is the quo has no status. Change happens. It either happens to us or because of us" (2008, paragraph 9). Now is the moment that we educators must seize control of our own destiny, lest someone else seize it for us.

A first step in wresting back this control is regaining public confidence and trust. Many of the attacks from the critics of public education (discussed in more depth in chapter 3) have legitimacy, but privatization is not the answer. Rather, the case for public education in America is as strong as ever. Indeed, for the twentieth century it was sufficient to provide a basic education for the majority of the population, thus preparing them for a low-skilled workforce that still offered access to the American dream and a middle-class lifestyle.

For the twenty-first-century citizen and workforce, that goal is no longer sufficient. Rather, what was once the purveyance of a more educated elite has become a necessity for all. Access to the American dream is growing ever out of reach for low-skilled workers. The need for an educated citizenry is higher than ever before, and this demands a greater need from our public education, quite the antithesis of the clamors to do away with it. The overriding purpose of public education is largely unchanged from its formation two centuries ago. How that purpose is manifested needs to drastically change.

Shattering Tradition

We must shatter tradition to maintain continuity with the past. To achieve the original purpose of education in the twenty-first-century context, it is no longer business as usual. As we discussed in chapter 1, there are two primary purposes for education: survival and understanding. For modern society, that survival purpose is primarily to generate a citizen who contributes to society and the workforce. Survival for the twenty-first century is entirely different than at any other point in history. The knowledge and skills we have handed down for the last two centuries are no longer sufficient.

Moreover, we may not be biologically prepared for the world we live in. The human body evolved to meet very different survival needs than we face in modern society. For example, our craving for fatty foods was a good thing in our earlier human history. Eating fatty foods in a hunting and gathering society, when food was scarcer, meant we could store much needed energy and it increased our odds of making it until the next meal came along. Now, in a time of abundance, our craving for fatty foods has led to a high incidence of obesity, diabetes, and heart disease. Robert Sapolsky (2004) goes in depth into the phenomenon of our outdated biology in his book *Why Zebras Don't Get Ulcers*.

Sapolsky highlights how our engrained fight or flight response system, a survival instinct that has helped our species survive for thousands of years, is now leading to harmful stress and actually hindering our ch,ances for survival. Those stress responses are vital when an animal encounters a predator or enemy; however, they are detrimental to a person stuck in rush hour traffic twice a day every day.

As we have discussed, the second purpose for learning is rooted in more abstract thought and the brain's natural instinct to ask "why?" This learning as a means of satisfying curiosity also seems to be innate. Twenty-first-century education must nurture both of these learning purposes in a balanced manner. Past education was more focused on the first purpose, survival. Modern education will need to continue to meet the survival purpose for education while integrating and fostering a deeper understanding of the abstract; a love of learning for its own sake.

The educational system of the past really only needed to advance the first purpose for the majority and could reserve the second purpose for the elite few. This is no longer the case.

One hundred years ago Albert Einstein shattered the traditional Newtonian understanding of gravity when he published his Theory of Relativity. For centuries, Sir Isaac Newton's equations served as the accepted model for physicists everywhere. Einstein's new equation, $E=MC^2$, suggested things were much trickier. For the past century, this theory has been tested time and time again and continues to hold true even with all the new knowledge gained in this time.

Einstein's radical work maintained continuity with the past's goal of creating mathematical models to predict and accurately measure observations of the cosmos. Modern physicists and astronomers continue to utilize and test his theory of relativity searching for the elusive unified theory that can explain all the known forces of the universe. Einstein's initially controversial work changed the game for astronomy and physics one hundred years ago.

Modern education needs a similar game changer. Unlike gravity, however, the game of education cannot be changed with a mathematical formula discovered by one man and tested by several men and women over a century. To change the model of education will take a systemic effort on the part of many. It will take a type of crowd-sourcing.

For our return to greatness, we must shatter the entrenched and engrained twentieth-century tradition to maintain continuity with the past ideals of public education. Just as Einstein's theory maintained continuity with the past ideals of Galileo and Newton, education must maintain continuity with the past ideals of Plato and Jefferson. True, by today's standards, the Platonic and Jeffersonian models are outdated. Yet, for their respective period, they were revolutionary. That is what we need now, another revolution within public schools. Mere reform is not enough.

The Revolution Will Not Be Standardized

The next chapter will delve deeper into the attacks on our current system, and it is important to distinguish one fact between the assertions of this book and the assertions of many of public education's detractors: we must not throw the baby out with the bathwater. There is a concerted effort pushing for increased standardization and privatization of education. This is not the answer. Indeed it is quite the opposite. America's public education system is becoming ever more crucial to our sustainability as a nation. Unfortunately, we may be down the wrong path—the path of ever increasing standardization. As Zhao (2012) observes:

> the traditional education paradigm may have worked before but it is no longer adequate for the changed world. The efforts

to develop common curriculum, nationally and internationally, are simply working to perfect an outdated paradigm. The outcomes are precisely the opposite of the talents we need for the new era. It is the wrong bet for our children's future. (p. 45)

The ideals of federal initiatives such as No Child Left Behind and Race to the Top are hard to argue against; the reality of their methods, however, may do more harm than good. Similar to Newton's explanation of gravity, their time has passed.

So what exactly are the goals of the traditional paradigm? As we look forward, it is important to take a moment to look back. We must select with what part of the past we choose to maintain continuity. We must examine the greatness to which we wish to return.

Maintaining Continuity

While early founders of our democracy such as Thomas Jefferson and Horace Mann advocated strongly for public education, there is nothing in the U.S. Constitution that creates such an institution. Rather, public education falls under the Tenth Amendment (1791): "The powers not delegated to the United States by the Constitution, nor prohibited by it to the States, are reserved to the States respectively, or to the people." It is not by accident that all fifty states have a provision for public education within their state constitution.

Alexis de Tocqueville observed the strong foundation that public education provided for our young nation when he traveled the country in 1835. Over the years, public education has served as a beacon of upward mobility, offering, with varying degrees of success, equal opportunity for the American dream. And while it doesn't fall under its legal jurisdiction, the federal government has long taken an interest in the education of the nation.

From Supreme Court cases to the original establishment of the U.S. Department of Education in 1867 to No Child Left Behind and the Common Core, this growing interest is readily apparent.

And while the makeup of the U.S. Department of Education has looked different over the years, its stated mission remains "to promote student achievement and preparation for global competitiveness by fostering educational excellence and ensuring equal access" (U.S. Department of Education, n.d.).

The Future Is the Brain

While it is impossible to predict the future, it is a safe bet that in education, the twenty-first century will be about the brain. With advancements in technology, an ever-flattening world, and new learning about the human brain, education will need to move toward a more personalized, growth mindset and away from the current standardized, fixed mindset. This will be an important shift for three major reasons: (1) standardization isn't real—it's a fabricated illusion, (2) technology advances are changing the way we live: simultaneously connecting and disconnecting us in newer ways, and (3) there is an ever-increasing need for individuals to be nimble—the way Kodak was not.

Education must build on the brain's natural tendencies to build connections. Artficial intelligence (AI) is developing in greater ways to more accurately mirror the way the original supercomputer, the human brain, learns and grows. Education must tap the potential of the human brain not just to develop better AI, but to also develop better natural intelligence. The factory model of standardization will not accomplish this.

The Standardized Illusion

The standardized model of education is an artificially imposed order forced upon a more abstract process. Standardization is great for manufacturing. Indeed it has its origins in the factory line. However, now that our economy has moved from the Industrial Age into the Information Age, this standardized model is outdated.

Moreover, it is unnatural. Straight lines do not exist within the wild, but that is all you see in suburban landscaping. There is order in nature and in the universe and new scientific research is highlighting this, but this cosmic order is very different than the one imposed upon nature by humankind. The twenty-first-century model of education must embrace these new (and not so new) findings. The Cartesian model served its purpose and now it is time for us to expand and evolve in our worldview. If we do not, we risk breeding a brain-dead, zombie culture.

Zombie Factories

Popular culture has been fascinated with zombies for over a decade now. Sure, zombies have always been a staple of the horror genre, but more than just a staple, zombies have been at the forefront of American pop culture since the movie *28 Days Later* hit theaters in 2002. Since then there have been several other box office hits, bumper stickers, gag gifts, and even a zombie Christmas Carol book (Spradlin, 2009). The hit series *The Walking Dead* is in its sixth season. Why has America's typically short attention span been focused on zombies for so long? Perhaps they are symbolic of our collective daydream.

The popularity of zombies may reflect the often soulless nature of modern society. Indeed, the more connected we become through technology, the more disconnected we become with our fellow humans, our family, and friends at the organic level. For example, current studies are finding a high correlation between Facebook usage and depression.

Our students are entering schools with greater socioemotional deficits, especially those from high poverty. Our brains did not evolve for this type of interfacing. Rather we are biologically hard-wired, if you will, for face-to-face interaction. New research with the hormone oxytocin is illustrating this fact. We have a biological imperative for human connection. The great American author Kurt Vonnegut often asserted that modern society's ills were attributed to the breakdown of the extended family.

Voices from the Field

Every educator knows that the students who enter their classroom are unique. Teachers understand that not all students learn the same way. They understand that with each student comes a set of individual beliefs and experiences that affect how they learn and what they learn. As professionals in the education field we know that we need to differentiate our teaching style so that we include all types of learners. The knowledge that we as educators need to adjust our curriculum and our presentation styles to meet the needs of our students is nothing new.

We all do it, we have to do it, and we want to do it. Just as educators adjust their everyday strategies in the classroom based on the needs of students. So should the American education system adjust to the needs of our society?

I believe that schools need to move forward into the twenty-first century by focusing on the whole child. The definition of the "whole child" can be interpreted as a child's body, mind, and soul. By soul I do not mean in the religious sense. I simply mean the emotional health of our students. The American educational system needs to put less value on high-stakes testing and more value on how we educate our students and what skills we need them to learn.

I am not saying that assessments are not valuable or necessary. I am simply saying that as we move forward we need to prioritize creating functional adults and creative thinkers who are prepared to enter a constantly changing global world, full of social issues rather than be driven by the outcome of high-stakes testing. Creating a school environment that is more flexible can allow professionals in the educational field to use creative solutions in the classroom, and allow teachers to embrace what we refer to as "teachable moments." The present model allows very little flexibility due to fear that students will fail to do well on these high-stakes tests.

Schools can help foster solutions to our world's social problems by providing opportunities for social growth, by giving students experience interacting with their peers and their communities in positive ways that reflect change; hoping to inspire students to stay connected to their community and facilitate civic responsibility that will help make our world a better place. It is also the responsibility of our educational system to help students learn how to take care of their bodies by helping them understand how to grow, harvest, and prepare nutritious and healthy foods.

Schools also need to educate students on how to stay physically active and the importance of staying active; helping to curb the obesity epidemic that is sweeping our nation. Schools can get involved in school gardening projects and form a farm-to-school committee. Schools can provide students with the knowledge of where their food comes from and the importance of nourishing their bodies so that they can nourish their minds. Thus, sharing the importance of taking care of our earth as a nation, we can grow food sustainably and responsibly.

Finally, our schools need to be places that foster safe creative learning. The education system needs to provide students with multiple experiences in flexible classrooms that help them learn to problem solve, persevere, and develop an innate curiosity. Schools need to provide global experiences, by using technology tools such as epals (I have had wonderful experiences using this host site) or Google Earth that prepare them for working in a global society.

As educators we will have to retrain our thinking and the way we have been taught to teach. I look at this as a challenge, a good one and a necessary one. Educators will need to learn to prioritize teaching students to synthesize, analyze, and evaluate problems. Incorporating hands-on academic challenges that cultivate critical thinking in our students. Teachers will have to move off of the stage and take a new role as facilitator. Allowing students time to explore and allowing them to fail and then asking them to try again.

As a society we need to ask ourselves what will the adults of the future need to know? What social problems will they need to solve? Equipping our students with critical thinking skills, confidence, and the desire to create effective and humanitarian change will allow them to move toward solving any future issues and hopefully be productive members of society. If we can move our educational system into the twenty-first century and beyond, we can quite possibly help our students succeed in a future we know very little about.

—Georgia Holt,
Gallatin Gateway School District,
Bozeman, Montana

Rapid Technology, Slow Biology

It takes one hundred years to change a value. This presents a real challenge when technology is growing so rapidly. Our biology can't keep up either. Indeed, our education system is better suited for one hundred years ago. The question exists: will these rapid technological advances enhance us as a society and species or will they merely magnify and intensify our flaws?

Take a moment to think about all the great advancements with medicine, communication, travel, and so on, and how they have enhanced our lives. Now think about technology's impact with cyberbullying, pornography, terrorism, identity theft, child exploitation, and pedophilia. Lest we get too doom and gloom, there are signs of hope for the future generation. The millenials, while generally more narcissistic and entitled than older generations, are more positive and optimistic in their outlook on life. To build on this positivity and optimism and to address the challenges of our modern world, we propose a container model for twenty-first-century education.

The Education Crucible

The modern public school is in search of its identity. Caught between two worlds, leaders are struggling to meet the modern needs of their students within an antiquated system. To help get us through this, it's time for every student's favorite subject: recess! Ever wonder why children love recess so much? Of course, not! It's obvious—play is fun.

But even though play is fun, it isn't frivolous or wasteful. Rather, brain research demonstrates just how much work play really is. Indeed, play is the workplace of the child learner. Play is nature's school. Our twenty-first-century school will do well to borrow a chapter from play therapy's playbook—pun intended.

Play therapy is a structured environment that allows for and creates flexibility, exploration, creativity, and work. Within the structure, the child is free to explore, to learn, and to make connections. Guided by a trained professional, this child-centered (learner-centered) milieu facilitates the individual's natural proclivity to learn, grow, and self-renew. For a wonderful case study of the transformative power of play therapy, see the seminal work *Dibs In Search of Self* (Axline, 1964).

This same container model that helps children work through emotional and psychological issues can be employed for our schools as well. John Hunter's *World Peace Game* (2013) is an excellent example of this phenomenon in action in a school setting. Mr. Hunter's lesson with public school fourth graders provides an excellent example of what can happen when educators work to facilitate growth and learning instead of control it. Likewise, chess is a game that has demonstrated educational benefits (Barrett & Fish, 2011). This is the new direction for education. Chapter 4 will expand on how this container model can promote a holistic, comprehensive accountability as an alternative to our current punishment model.

Fujifilm Flashback

We'll conclude this chapter similiar to how we began. This time, however, we will look at Kodak's rival Fujifilm. Like Kodak, Fujifilm held a near monopoly in its home market, Japan. Likewise, Fulifilm's main products, cameras and film, became obsolete with the development of new technology. The big difference? While Kodak is reeling from this shift in the market, Fujifilm is still posting large profits. How is this possible? Like Kodak, Fujifilm saw the writing on the wall, but unlike Kodak they did something about it. They adapted.

Fujifilm diversified its business and reconstructed its business model. This wasn't an easy process. Indeed, it was very controversial and rife with internal conflict. It also went against the grain of Japanese corporate culture, which is typically very tradition rich and change resistant. It took vision, dedication, and a willingness to make unpopular decisions by Fujifilm's leader, Shigetaka Komori. While these types of actions were contrary to the cultural norm, one cultural benefit Fujifilm did have over Kodak was corporate Japan's long-term culture. That is, shareholders were more interested in the long-term payoffs than the short-term. In American corporate culture, this is often not the case.

For American public education to survive in the twenty-first century, it needs to pay heed to the lessons of Kodak and Fujifilm. Educational leaders are at a crossroads and have a choice to make: hold on to a dying model and go down with the ship like Kodak, or radically transform our business model and prepare for the future like Fujifilm. Our vision for education is one for the long term.

References

Axline, V. M. (1964). *Dibs in search of self.* New York: Ballantine Books.

Barrett, D. C. & Fish W. W. (2011). Our move: Using chess to improve math achievement for students who receive special education services. *The International Journal of Special Education, 26*(3), 181-193.

Houston, P. D. (2008, May). Wherever you go. *The School Administrator,* 5(65). Retrieved from http://aasa.org/SchoolAdministratorArticle.aspx?id=5400

Hunter, J. (2013). *World peace and other 4th grade achievements.* New York, NY: Houghton Mifflin Harcourt Publishing Company.

Johnson, S. (1998). *Who moved my cheese? An amazing way to deal with change in your work and in your life.* New York: G.P. Putnam's Sons.

McCammon, S. (September, 2013). The end of Kodak moments? *NPR Marketplace.* Retrieved from http://www.marketplace.org/topics/business/end-kodak-moments

O'Connor, F. (1952). *Wise blood.* New York: Harcourt, Brace & Company.

Rao, R. (2014, July 24). What Xerox can learn from Kodak's disintegration and Fuji's re-invention. Retrieved from http://www.zdnet.com/what-xerox-can-learn-from-kodaks-disintegration-and-fujis-re-invention-7000031971/

Sapolsky, R. (2004). *Why zebras don't get ulcers,* 3rd ed. New York: Henry Holt and Company.

Spradlin, M. P. (2009). *It's beginning to look a lot like zombies. A book of zombie Christmas carols.* New York: Harper.

The Economist. (2012, January 14). The last Kodak moment? Retrieved from http://www.economist.com/node/21542796

U.S. Department of Education (n.d.). What we do. Retrieved from http://ww2.ed.gov/about/what-we-do.html

Zhao, Y. (2012). *World class learners: Educating creative and entrepreneurial students.* Thousand Oaks, CA: Corwin Press.

3

The War on American Public Education

> Don't let anyone tell you that standardized tests are not accurate measures. The truth of the matter is they offer a remarkably precise method for gauging the size of the houses near the school where the test is administered.
>
> —Alfie Kohn, *Fighting the Tests: A Practical Guide to Rescuing Our Schools*

Learning is innate; it is natural. Learning will occur with or without formal education. Yet, what we formally teach, when we teach it, where we teach it, how we teach it, and to whom we teach it are some of the most controversial topics in our nation. This basic controversy is not new. Public education in the United States has experienced criticism and controversy since its inception. Modern debates about the role of religion, funding, equity, qualified teachers, and discipline have been divisive issues since at least the late eighteenth century.

Further, a historical overview of our public education system yields a host of inequalities, ineffective practices, and other blemishes. The importance of education as a means of preparing youth for and creating access to full participation in society means that removing these blemishes and creating the best system possible is vital to a thriving democracy. It also lends itself to varying opinions of how to best accomplish this. It also lends itself to competition of resources.

As we stated, these things are not new. What is new is the personal tone the controversy and criticisms are now taking. The tone has moved beyond simple advocacy for change or criticism of how the system is being run. Now, the critics are attacking the profession itself. Today's criticism has become so harsh and so pervasive that the term "war" may be a better description.

The Sputnik Syndrome

The tone began to change in the 1950s when the Soviet Union launched the Sputnik satellite into space. With our Cold War rivals taking the lead in the space race, the perceived failure was placed on our public school system. Why had the Soviets taken the lead in this competition? It must have been due to a superior school system. In the wake of this crisis, *Life Magazine* (1958) launched a three-part series titled "Crisis in Education."

The first issue featured a photo essay comparing and contrasting two sixteen-year-old boys, each intended to represent a typical high school student in his country: Alexei Kutzkov of Moscow and Stephen Lapekas of Chicago. The photo essay paints a picture of a Soviet school system that is serious and demands academic success and an American system that is less serious and more relaxed. While Alexei strives to learn the most he can in school, Stephen jokes around in class. While Alexei conducts serious physics experiments, Stephen practices the latest dance craze. While Alexei studies fervently into the night, Stephen spends his time enjoying sports and talking with girls.

The Soviet educational system was heralded for its emphasis on academic rigor:

> With a curriculum standardized across the country and with no elective subjects, the Soviet 10-year schools are like mammoth obstacle courses for the nation's youth. The laggards are forced out by tough periodic examinations and shunted

to less demanding trade schools and apprenticeships. Only a third—1.4 million in 1957—survive all 10 years and finish the course. (p. 27)

Hmm, does any of that sound familiar?

A Nation at Risk?

If the seeds for the current war on public education were planted in 1957, they really took root in 1983 when the federal government issued *A Nation at Risk* (National Commission on Excellence in Education, 1983). Our present-day educational policy is still reeling from the aftershocks of this impactful, scathing report.

Once again, the fear-mongers were predicting the downfall of America due to its lackluster public education system. Widespread reforms were invoked and it was time for America's schools to buckle down and return to rigor or face a world dominated by the Communists. The 1980s also invoked a threat from Japan and the fear that its economy would overpower ours. The problem there was seen to be our lazy workforce, products of a soft educational system.

Yet, despite these outcries, despite the wailing and gnashing of teeth, America won the Cold War. It was the USSR that collapsed, not the United States. Contrary to the fear-mongers' predictions, communism did not take over the planet, nor did Japan take over the U.S. economy.

How are these things possible if our public school system is so evil? The critics are quick to scapegoat public schools for the perceived faults or weaknesses of our nation, yet the converse is never seen. Never do you hear pundits praising public schools when our economy is strong. When the Soviet Union collapsed and the Berlin Wall came down, did anyone point to America's public schools and give credit to our educators? No.

Make no mistake, we are not attributing such successes to public education, merely pointing out the fallacy of such attacks. If public education is responsible for our nation's failures, it only logically follows that it should likewise be responsible for our nation's successes. Yet, the critics don't ever give credit, they only lay blame. Indeed, the last sixty years of attacks have fueled an ongoing blame game.

This game pits parents against teachers, teachers against administrators, students against teachers, legislators against educators, and so on. In a realm where the majority of participants are striving for the same goal, rather than collaborating to overcome obstacles, each party villainizes the other. Senge (2006) described a similar dynamic played out in the business scenario known as "the beer game" (p. 27). Instead of administrators, teachers, and students, the beer game features the retailer, the wholesaler, and the brewery. You can see the parallels here:

> People in the business world love heroes. We lavish praise and promotion on those who achieve visible results. But if something goes wrong, we feel intuitively that somebody must have screwed up.
>
> In the beer game, there are no such culprits. There is no one to blame. Each of the three players in our story has the best possible intentions: to serve his customers well, to keep the product moving smoothly through the system, and to avoid penalties. Each participant made well-motivated, clearly defensible judgments based on reasonable guesses about what might happen. There were no villains, but there was a crisis nonetheless—built into the structure of the system. (pp. 40–41)

Similarly, public education needs champions who can rise above these petty games and help transform the structure of the system instead of looking for scapegoats.

Competition

Whether you agree or disagree with *A Nation at Risk*, there is no denying it had a great impact on American public schools. Some of the impact was predictable while some was not. While public and private schools have competed for students over the last century, *A Nation at Risk* clearly brought about more competition for students (predicted) and ultimately competition for public monies (not predicted). It brought about a need for better accountability (predicted), which does not recognize all of the important work public schools do and the public needs them to do (not predicted).

And of course, all of this increased the role politics would play in public schools (predicted) resulting in a movement for public dollars to pay for private alternatives (unpredicted). No one should have been surprised that the attack *A Nation at Risk* made on the public education system would result in more alternatives for education consumers. Prior to the 1980s, the biggest competition for the public school was a variety of private schools, many of which were tied to religious organizations.

While we are strong advocates of the American public school system, make no mistake, we not only strongly believe in competition but also believe that the rigor of the competition is necessary for the American public school to thrive and return to greatness! The competition since *A Nation at Risk* has already improved the job we do and raised standards for student performance.

As of the fall of 2015, most measures of any significance would suggest that the highest percentage of school-age children in the United States chose a nontraditional public school option than at any time in the history of the public school system. What should be alarming to professional educators is that this trend has continued every year since the publication of *A Nation at Risk* in 1983. During this time, not only has the number of private schools increased, but so has the number of charter schools and for-profit schools and the number of children being homeschooled. The trend is projected by the Department of Education to continue for the foreseeable future.

Consequently, homeschooling research predicts that by 2025 one out of every four school-age children in the United States will be schooled at home or within the expanding homeschool network. Private school endowments are at record levels, yet they generally offer similar benefits of public schools with one exception: a substantially higher perceived value by the consuming public. If you pay extra for it, it must be better! Right? States continue to approve more open enrollment charter schools, and for-profit enterprises have used the charter school movement as an entry into for-profit schools paid for with public money.

Many of these new alternatives do a very good job while others have been failures and a waste of taxpayer money. Jones (2013) explains this trend as a loss of marketshare:

> As educators, we do not like to think of ourselves as being in business or that we compete for customers, but the reality is that we are and we do. If our public school consumer was satisfied with what we had to offer, then obviously there would be little or no need for the alternatives those consumers are choosing.
>
> Moreover, the reality of this decline in public school market share has enormous implications. In business, a continuing decline in market share ultimately leads to the inability of the organization to sustain itself. Take General Motors as a perfect example. For many years, although profitable, General Motors continued to lose market share as their business model failed to compete in a changing market. Twenty years ago, no one would have predicted bankruptcy for the once largest corporation in the world, yet in 2009 they filed bankruptcy which led to fundamental change to that business model including substantial downsizing. (p. 11)

General Motors downsized and changed its business model to compete by regaining marketshare and thus reverse the trend. By 2014, General Motors was once again growing its marketshare and making money again. General Motors had effectively changed to compete also in an arena of increased competition and number of manufacturers innovating to meet market needs. How long can the American public school continue to lose marketshare before its viability becomes in jeopardy. Who profits or loses if American public schools fail? Who profits or loses if they succeed?

Does the increase in competition or trend in loss of marketshare set the stage for public school obsolescence or does it unleash an opportunity for it to strive for a new level of importance and return to greatness? Can the American public school system mount a recovery like General Motors or has the dye been cast for it to be the next American Motors? Obviously if we believed in the latter we wouldn't be writing this book as we believe no educational enterprise has the capacity for greatness more so than the American public school.

High-Stakes Testing

Accountability is a critical component of any enterprise focused on excellence or quality and in education that accountability logically includes testing. Our consumers who fund our endeavors deserve to know what students are learning (curriculum) and to what extent they have mastered that learning (performance). Teachers have been testing since the one-room schoolhouse; and as other educational endeavors of the world became more competitive, the need for a widespread standardized approach for testing emerged.

There is no evidence that performance standards of schools will not continue to rise as they consistently have since *A Nation at Risk*. With the passage of No Child Left Behind (2002), there is a compelling national interest for that trend to continue for the foreseeable future. Would anyone want to be responsible for lowering standards? Ultimately the public, through its representatives, wants more from the funds it provides and for the education profession to be accountable for that task. This, in and of itself, is not a bad thing.

Hence, more robust testing was a predictable outcome of *A Nation at Risk*. What was not predictable was an accountability system that largely was informed exclusively by testing and that the primary judge of a student's performance would be reduced to his or her performance on one of two days in the spring of each year. Parents and the American public expect far more from the public school than instruction and mastery of the formal curriculum. They expect high school graduates to be well adjusted members of society and with the human and interpersonal skills necessary for amalgamating into the larger social system.

Voices from the Field

Twenty plus years in the corporate accounting world fueled my passion for what I really enjoyed about my job: teaching and guiding others. When the opportunity came for a full-time career in teaching, I jumped on it. In 2004 I obtained my alternative certification, then began working as a fifth grade math teacher.

Working with young people to ignite their passion for learning about math brought about the start of an exciting adventure in the hardest job I have ever had. I've been fortunate to teach with an amazing team of professionals supported by an administration and district that truly puts children first. However, I know now that my experience in private industry and as a parent of two boys couldn't really prepare me for all the challenges and plate juggling this profession requires.

For the last ten years as an educator, I have served in many roles in addition to "just" teaching the prescribed curriculum: disciplinarian, referee, mentor, cheerleader, and psychologist as well as school and district level committee responsibilities. However, I soon realized that serving these multiple roles while teaching three to four classes of seventy-five to one hundred students per year of different backgrounds, priorities, and abilities was going to become tenfold the job I had as a parent. And I had to get these students to excel academically while keeping them engaged and on task. And I had to manage the expectations and communications with the parents of these students, my coworkers, and my administration.

At the beginning of my teaching career the state standardized test had just changed to become a more challenging assessment of student learning. Doing well on this test was important to the school and the district's accountability ratings. Although the expectation at my school was that all students would pass this test, the better the students performed the better rating our school received.

So, my ultimate responsibility was to make sure these kids performed their best on the **one** state testing day. That one day performance could make or break the school, district, or perhaps the teacher. And in fifth grade they had to pass the math portion and my class to be promoted to sixth grade. No pressure and a simple task, right?

Managing these ten- and eleven-year-old children in an organized, structured, and productive environment to gear them toward success on *this **one day** was my challenge. Why wouldn't every child love to be in a high-performing school with excellent teachers in a nurturing environment? Certainly off-task behavior could be easily redirected!! Wrong—sort of. I quickly realized that a good work ethic, love of learning, and healthy home environment were not necessarily the norm—regardless of income bracket. Most kids would follow my lead.*

But when dealing with people, and especially children, there are a million reasons why the instruction, or students' desire or ability to do as they are asked, doesn't always go as planned. There is always the kid who wants to be the rebel, or did not eat breakfast, or fought with a sibling before school, or hated his or her teacher last year and doesn't like math, or needs frequent breaks, or doesn't have parents who look over his or her homework or even make sure it was done.

*The multiple roles I served as a teacher to meet this **one day** testing goal was at least equal to the different learning styles and learning accommodations my students needed. How could I as a teacher make sure my students were getting everything they needed? How did I focus attention on students that needed extra help while keeping the others engaged and learning? What about the student who needed a stress ball to handle attention deficit disorder or needed a weighted vest to manage anxiety and anger? What about the gifted and talented students who needed to be challenged? What about the student who missed my class a couple of times a week to receive dyslexia services? How could I make sure the activities and assessments were at a level that would ensure success? What about the English learners (ELs) that were now becoming part of my assessment as a teacher? Could I explain why a student did well on classroom tests but "bombed" the district benchmarks, or vice versa?*

The expectation and measures for student success have only grown and become more comprehensive throughout my ten years in teaching with continual "new and improved" state assessments and methodologies for evaluating schools and districts. I think the changes have been made with good intentions. However, every transition has put the cart before the horse—the state education agency announces the general changes, then follows up months later with specific details in the middle of the school year.

(continued)

> This creates a counterproductive, time intensive guessing game on how the state will assess the curriculum. Poor communication from and untimely decisions by the state education agency result in teachers spending valuable time finding updated lesson and classroom assessment resources. Throw a new textbook adoption into the mix along with a significant realignment to the math curriculum to help create an increasingly frustrating work environment.
>
> Finally, none of these issues even addresses the effects of new technology, changing demographics of families, increasing number of school related meetings, increasing documentation required for struggling students, RTI meetings, ARDs, 504s, and the like. Or, the students who get checked out of school early. Or, the students who are left alone after school because both their parents work and they don't get their homework done or don't prepare for tests. Or, the students who don't qualify for special education but display learning struggles. Or, the countless hours spent lesson planning, grading papers, searching for engaging lesson ideas, or calling parents in the evenings about their child's struggles.
>
> So is teaching rewarding? Absolutely. Hearing my student say "I get it!" performing well on a test, watching them help each other understand a concept, or giving me a hug in the morning—these are all great moments. However, unless you have walked in a teacher's shoes with all the daily pressures and responsibilities of a young person's future in their hands, don't assume that it is an easy job with summers off. I spend most of my summers preparing for the challenges of the next year!
>
> —Judith Neimann Black,
> Conroe Independent School District
> Conroe, Texas

Most state constitutions place the burden of developing good democratic citizens on the state-funded education system. Yet none of these informal curricular tasks are included in any form of testing and therefore do not reflect in the accountability of most public schools. Only in an American public school are any and all children welcome to attend and utilize the multitude of academic, social, and psychological services they might need.

Hence, accountability for American public schools has generally been reduced to a child's performance on a standardized test on a day or two in the spring. While all other alternatives have some ability to restrict or limit who attends (yes, even open enrollment charter schools limit the number of enrollees and can exit students at any time). Bring us your masses and we will educate them, but judge us solely on how those masses do on day two of testing for the year. That is what it means to employ high-stakes testing.

This inadequate form of accountability has become a significant attack on public education as it refuses to acknowledge the multitude of things the school does with great success and how those things are so critical to a democratic electorate and to a productive economy.

High-stakes testing addresses the questions of "what" we teach and "to what extent" students have mastered it. We believe in accountability and that testing for student performance plays a critical role in being held accountable. But we also believe our current accountability system needs to be reformed, and our return to greatness will require a more sophisticated system of authentic assessment that values and measures all the things a public school does in meeting the state and local community's mission. This area is so important to our return to greatness that chapter 4 has been devoted to it. Chapter 5 will explore "how" we teach as another critical element on our return to greatness.

Some international standardized tests indicate that the United States has lost intellectual dominance in the world marketplace. We believe this is important and more a byproduct of "how" we teach rather than "what" or "to what extent" we teach and master. That discussion will be addressed in chapter 5 but for now we want to make it clear that the American public school return to greatness will require a very individualized approach to higher performance on standardized tests and require a more comprehensive approach to assessment and accountability.

Politics and the Evolution of the School Voucher Movement

Educators generally hate politics when it comes to public schools! The only thing most educators hate more than politics is talking about it, which is why most professional educators have little involvement in public policy formulation or the politics necessary to influence it. Some states have unions to do that for educators, but what most of the general public does not know is that all but about a dozen states and the overwhelming majority of public school educators are *not* members of a union and have no part of their employment negotiated on their behalf or benefit from a collective bargaining agreement! Politicians and the media would have you believe differently but are simply misrepresenting the facts either unintentionally or perhaps intentionally. (Okay, we said it!)

The inadequate testing and accountability system in most states have fueled some politicians in touting that our publicly funded schools are failing our children. Moreover, the attacks are now personally launched at educators, accusing them of being inadequate, too expensive, overly entitled, and generally mediocre at best.

We wonder where all these critics were educated and how they developed their skills for ascending into such powerful positions? School choice after *A Nation at Risk* meant public alternatives for the state to still meet its education mandate required in every state constitution. The more competition that has ensued, the more attacks have been levied on public schools and professional educators in their employ. Most of these realities were probably predictable in the days following *A Nation at Risk*.

What no one foresaw was the proliferation of extreme political think tanks and their supporting politicians that parlayed "school choice" to mean publicly funded private schools. Some of these groups, and the politicians that receive money from them, campaigned for school choice as a means for giving parents the ability to use public money to attend any school they want.

Seemingly this would include the most prestigious schools in any city. Who would not want to send their child, for example, to the school that yields the most national merit scholars or the most nominations to one of the military academies. This phenomenon was illustrated in Jones (2013) as the Everyone Can Go to Harvard Theory:

With a voucher program, parents in theory could put their child in any school they wish and the vast sums of money, both state funds and local property tax money, would follow the child in whatever option was selected. In theory, parents could use state money to place their child in the most prestigious private school in the community. Of course, that isn't possible and would result in many students (mostly intellectually and economically advantaged) leaving the public school system on a quest for something more prestigious or better perceived school while stripping critical resources from the public school system. School vouchers are a recipe for crippling the public school system by redistributing public money into other educational alternatives that provide little evidence (other than perception) of their effectiveness in educating all students or providing the best environments for learning. (pp. 11–12)

While this attack on public education may be the most serious threat to its survival, it is also the threat that impedes its capacity to return to greatness. If the public, through its publicly elected representatives, wants to strip away the resources that fund it to place it into private endeavors, then so be it as that is democracy.

Hence, our return to greatness will require educators to be better marketers and communicators and no longer can we stay out of the political and public policy arena. Too many educators see the public education enterprise in terms of their career and not in terms of organizational survival.

School leaders will have to step up and take on the difficult challenges of our return to greatness and not just be complacent that the system will last "until I retire" (thus feeding and supporting the entitled educator argument). We cannot continue to watch the decline in marketshare making that reality our legacy. To do nothing to reverse the trend is the same as contributing to the decline in the first place. In our return to greatness, not only must we demonstrate that a public education is the best option for a family sending their child to school, we had better realize that every year we fail to do it diminishes our capacity to reverse the trend at all.

To be absolutely clear: We believe in public schools and a public school education for all American children. These attacks on the industry we have given our lives to has not dissuaded us away from the incredible time-tested American public education system or its value and merits to our country, our economy, or our democracy.

So true that we have written this book as our belief that a public school education is not only a good choice for American families, but it is the best choice for developing the whole child and preparing him or her for a highly competitive and diverse world. It is for this reason we chart a course for the American public school return to greatness so that our students, their families, and all the other stakeholders see that it is the best choice too! If you can read this book, you should probably thank a public school teacher!

References

Crisis in education. (1958, March 24). *Life Magazine*, 44(12), 25–35.

Jones, T. B. (2013). *Education for the human brain: A roadmap to natural learning in schools.* Lanham, MD: Rowman & Littlefield.

National Commission on Excellence in Education. (1983). *A nation at risk: The imperative for educational reform.* Washington, DC: National Commission on Excellence in Education.

Senge, P. (2006). *The fifth discipline: The art and practice of the learning organization.* New York: Doubleday.

4
Comprehensive Accountability

> In the classroom, fierce allegiance to efficiency, short-term performance, and immediately measurable outcome result too often in the sacrifice of the experience of education on the altar of the product of education. In other words, the journey is often lost in the press for a destination.
>
> —Kathleen E. Fite and John L. Garcia,
> *A Perspective on Ritual: Toward a Direction for Revitalizing Learning Communities*

It's December, approaching the end of the first semester and with the cold weather, Ms. Ruiz's ninth grade culinary arts class is cooking chili using pressure cookers. The chili cook off is one of Ms. Ruiz's favorite projects each year. It gives the students a chance to experiment with different flavors and ingredients. It's also a great way for them to apply various techniques they've learned. The chili cook off is a competitive challenge for her beginning class. Compared with other dishes, chili allows students a creative way to demonstrate mastery in a manner that allows room for error.

For the sake of time and as part of their lesson unit, the students use pressure cookers. With the intense heat, the chili only takes twenty minutes to cook versus the two hours it takes for a traditional slow cook or simmer method. A pressure cooker is a great way to cook food quickly. It allows food to be cooked at a higher temperature than conventional boiling or steaming. In the process, the sealed pressure does not allow steam to escape and thus superheats the water.

With typical methods of boiling, water reaches 212 degrees Fahrenheit (100 degrees Celsius) and never rises due to excess heat vaporizing into steam. Within the pressure cooker, however, water can reach a temperature of 250 degrees Fahrenheit (121 Celsius). Trapping the heat in this container creates a system that allows for much faster cooking time. It's a great tool for Ms. Ruiz's chili cook off.

Down the hall from Ms. Ruiz's culinary arts classroom there is another pressure cooker at work in Ms. Jackson's math classroom. This intensity is not generated on the stovetop, however. Rather it is a product of the mounting pressures from above and below. From above, the state legislators, school district, and campus administration are increasing their pressure upon Ms. Jackson to raise student test scores.

From below the pressures of her job are increased by Ms. Jackson's students' high needs. Each year her students come to her with less of the socioemotional skills needed to navigate high school and succeed in math. Moreover, Ms. Jackson has witnessed the growth of the population of students from poverty and those students' corresponding increased nonacademic needs. She faces mounting pressure for classroom management and discipline coupled with increased class sizes and smaller budgets.

Each year the expectations placed on Ms. Jackson grow while her resources shrink and her students come to her with greater needs—both emotionally and academically. Ms. Jackson and thousands of teachers like her across the country are being squeezed in the middle. The temperature is rising and the end result will not be a tasty chili.

The Pressure Cooker School System

Under our current accountability system, our schools are becoming pressure cookers. This may be a good way to cook chili quickly, but it is not an effective model for educating students. The changing needs of the student population (highlighted in chapter 2) create pressure from below. The current legislation and accountability system create pressure from above. Sandwiched in between are our students and educators. They are being squeezed from above and below. This does not create an environment conducive to learning, quite the contrary.

Under stress, people regress. Instead of fostering learning and growth or promoting curiosity and a drive to succeed, this system creates a stressful and highly unpleasant environment for all. Sadly, this phenomenon is only getting worse. The state boards of education and the state legislatures giveth but they do not taketh away.

To illustrate this growing list of demands on our educators, Vollmer (2010) created a list of all that has been added to the plates of schools over the years. "Vollmer's list," as it has become known, illuminates all the additional responsibilities schools have taken on over the years in addition to teaching the "three Rs." And, rather than being given any credit for the myriad services provided, educators are instead blamed and attacked for every conceivable ill in society.

Our school accountability system is at a crossroads. The increased pressure of high-stakes testing is not only outdated, but harmful. Pressure cookers are not only utilized for cooking things fast, they have also been utilized as improvised explosive devices (IEDs), known as pressure cooker bombs. The pressure cooker that has become our accountability system is about to explode.

Indeed, many of public school's biggest critics would love to blow up the current system and replace it with privatization. This would be devastating for American democracy. Pressure can be good or pressure can be bad. The key for educational accountability in our return to greatness is to intentionally and effectively use pressure in a productive manner. We propose a container model for education to achieve that end. This container model is a new paradigm, it is a shift from a punishment model to a growth model.

Atonement versus Accountability

In many ways public education is atoning for past sins: a lack of accountability in the past and a history of discrimination have tarnished the reputation of public schools in the eyes of many. To atone for these sins, many have turned to legislation and litigation. It is self-evident how eager people are to sue in this country and, right or wrong, schools are often at the center of such litigation. Granted, positive effects such *Brown vs. Board of Education* and the Individuals with Disabilities Education Act (IDEA) have come from this power of the underserved.

However, the same power to heal can also destroy. Educational leaders and policies are often constrained by the fear of litigation. It will take brave leadership to chart a new path in the realm of accountability. While this leadership must work to correct the wrongs of the system (both past and present), it must do so in a manner that is corrective and not punitive. It definitely seems that much of the high-stakes testing and accountability measures take on a punitive tone. But punishment is not the answer because it punishes our future. We must learn to integrate these lessons of the past with a comprehensive, holistic, and sensible approach.

Everyone Is a Critic (and an Expert)

Education is an interesting arena. Because it is an arena where almost everyone has had a chance to play, it creates the unique situation wherein practically every citizen feels that he or she is an expert. This is not quite the case in other arenas, but given that almost everyone has gone to school, it gives people a sense of authority in this area that they likely don't feel in other fields. As David Sirota, senior writer for the *International Business Times*, has pointed out on Twitter, people who think that they are education policy experts because they went to school as kids is like people thinking they are medical experts because they went to the doctor (Sirota, 2014).

Yes, the public does call for safe hospitals, safe cars, and safe consumer products. Yet, in these circumstances, unlike with education, people don't tend to feel they are simultaneously medical experts or engineering experts. Because everyone is vested (financially via taxation and personally via family) and because everyone is an "expert," a transformation in education becomes quite a daunting task. It is impossible to please everyone; there will always be critics. The problem, however, is exacerbated when those verbose critics wield political and financial power.

Accountability versus Blame and Doubt

So what exactly does it mean to be accountable? To paraphrase Merriam-Webster's definition: to be accountable is to be answerable, to be able to explain. So, to whom is public education accountable? To whom does it answer? Quite simply, *public* education answers to the public it serves. Of course, *public* is a pretty broad term. Does that mean that the neighborhood elementary school answers only to its neighborhood? Or does it answer to its city, state, or nation?

And to whom in the public is it answerable? All people? All citizens? All tax-paying citizens? Philosophically, this debate could go on and on, but when wondering why things are the way they are, it is often best to follow the money. In this case, federal accountability is tied to federal funding (especially because they have no legal say-so over education).

At the state level, accountability can be viewed through a legal lens as well as financial one. Schools are also accountable at the local level through school districts and their governing school boards. Ultimately, however, holding educators accountable is important to protect each student's right to an education—this is protected by state constitutions. Likewise, because education is so vital to democracy, schools need to answer to the public at large regarding how they are preparing students to participate in our democracy.

We also know that what gets measured gets done. Therefore, it is clear that public schools need to answer to the public about (a) how they are spending the public's money and (b) how they are educating their children and future citizens. How this is done is vital. An effective accountability system will ensure that educators and students are doing their jobs. It will also empower them to do the best job they can. The current system, however, disempowers them. The current system is less about accountability and responsibility and more about punishment and blame.

Constructive criticism is a valuable tool for improvement. The key word, of course, is constructive. That is a critique that builds one up or presents material for one to build upon. Simple criticism or blame does not do this. The current high-stakes testing environment tends to promote more of the latter than the former. Sadly, this was not its intended case. After decades of zero accountability, initiatives like No Child Left Behind were intended to spur constructive criticism and help close achievement gaps.

But the devil is always in the details and much of the results do not align with the pronounced goals. Who can argue against a desire for all children to have the opportunity to succeed—to not be left behind? Yet, the results have simply been more of the same. Here it is 2015 and the goal was to achieve 100 percent by now. Instead, we have states constantly altering standards, filing for exemptions and playing a type of three-card, monte. Our accountability system has turned into a blame game where no one wins.

Change, Not Blame

When we blame, we do not change. Yet, how often do we witness educators laying the blame of student failure at the foot of the parents? Likewise, how often do parents return the blame? As in most cases, the truth lies somewhere in the middle. And, regardless of who truly is responsible for what, the end result is the same—a lose-lose situation. We want our students to take responsibility for their actions and for their education. We as adults—parents, educators, and community members—have to do the same.

There is a big difference between responsibility and blame. Holding education responsible (i.e., accountable) for spending time, money, and other resources is necessary and important. An effective accountability system will assess the progress of schools in achieving their goals and monitor their effective use of public resources. This effective accountability system will be comprehensive and part of the growth process that is education. An effective, comprehensive accountability system will foster responsibility, growth, and autonomy. Our current system overemphasizes blame, shame, and punishment for schools, teachers, and students alike.

How many people are successful in life despite their education instead of because of it? As the once harsh critic of public education Jamie Vollmer notes when he observed our current accountability system, "A strategy of blaming, demonizing, and intimidating educators was not only futile, it was counterproductive. Something had to change" (Vollmer, 2010, p. 38). The blame game must come to an end.

Holistic Accountability

One major change that will have significant impact is the accountability system. This new system will measure the skills that research shows students need to succeed in life. A new paradigm must come into practice in which accountability measures are embedded within the curriculum and daily learning. Many critics use a business model when recommending changes to education accountability.

But how many businesses measure their success with an arbitrary score once a year? None. Notwithstanding that the business paradigm has been demonstrated to be a poor model for education, even if we viewed our current high-stakes testing system through a business lens, it still doesn't hold water. Businesses measure their success with quarterly reports based on sales, growth, and productivity—in other words, multiple measures.

There is a bottom line, of course—profits. However, even profits are measured in context. Our current model doesn't reflect this approach. Thus, even if we were to accept the arguments of political and business pundits for treating schools like a business, then our accountability system still needs to change. This change is the container model.

Voices from the Field

After four decades in education, this I know to be true: (1) students really do want to learn and succeed, (2) teachers must be passionate about teaching, (3) strategies and methods continually change and often recycle under new names, and (4) accountability is society's way of proving success and, in the process, often creates stress for all parties.

It was a much different time when I began teaching. Accountability was embedded in the teaching process and not overly mentioned or openly emphasized. I do not remember feeling overloaded with paperwork, data management, or professional portfolios that documented my success as a teacher. I concentrated on great lesson design and the best ways to challenge students. Students were expected to complete work and demonstrate mastery, and progress was reported routinely.

Depending on the state, students were given standardized tests between second and fifth grades mainly for diagnostic purposes. Of course, high school students took either ACT or SAT tests in preparation for college. There was pressure to succeed: we had put man on the moon and the space shuttle program was well under way. Except for the oil crisis of the 1970s, life was good. I knew my teaching career would be long and successful. I had found my calling!

Somehow, toward the end of the twentieth century, demands changed and the focus shifted from student accomplishment to teacher accountability. The need to prove our global competiveness led to high-stakes testing, data-driven evaluations, a push for national, standards-based education, and a frenzied scramble to hold people accountable. In the process, teachers were held accountable for student success at a level not previously experienced. The intent was positive, but not necessarily the results. Under this pressure, thousands of veteran teachers struggled to justify continuing in a job they loved. The veterans felt out of control, and new teachers felt overwhelmed. Many left for other careers.

I believe accountability is necessary and fundamental to success. The trick is to create an accountability system that encourages excellence, is realistic, and does not create undo stress. In search of a realistic educational utopia, I have a few "what ifs":

1. What if we create a comprehensive method of assessing students that includes standardized testing along with performance products

and teacher/district created tests? This would encourage teaching that emphasizes critical thinking, student discussion, problem- and project-based learning, and real-world application.
2. *What if we design a program that provides time for veteran teachers to work with teachers entering the field or those needing the expertise of others to learn how to work within accountability systems?* We are all under pressure to do more with less. Yet, somehow, many teachers continue to put their passion for learning and student success first. These teachers do not let accountability programs overtake their mastery of the classroom. We cannot lose these great teachers to retirement or other careers before they pass along keys to success.
3. *What if we change the emphasis of state mandated tests?* We have taught parents and students that the single, state designated test is more important than all other assessments. If we use a system where students are evaluated using a combination of assessments, we can better gauge mastery of knowledge. Not all students are great test takers and to label a student based on one test is grossly unfair and invalid. Let's return to teaching content, not test-taking skills.
4. *What if teachers are held accountable through a variety of indicators?* I believe all teachers really do welcome feedback and want administrators to see how they teach; it is the validation of our efforts. How that is done determines the attitude of a school and ultimately the success of students. Can we create an atmosphere where administrators have continual contact in classrooms, maybe even interacting with students in lessons?

I am sure many teachers would welcome opportunities to showcase their teaching and student progress. This could also open doors for dialog and discussions, resulting in school wide improvements in morale and student success. Teacher accountability has taken a major turn toward goal setting, data collection to support these goals, and student progress tied to teacher evaluations. This is fine as long as teacher evaluation is not overly dependent on the standardized tests.

We need to look at the big picture with accountability.

—Cindy Burns, Hanovet County
Public Schools, Ashland, Virginia

The Education Crucible Returns

One of the primary obstacles to facilitating truly personalized learning is the overemphasis on standardized, high-stakes tests. Standardized measures have their place; however, balance is needed. As the futurist Gary Marx (2014) wrote,

> Let's admit it. On the one hand, standards can be helpful. Formative testing can guide us toward more personal learning and maybe even higher achievement. On the other hand, standards and standardized tests can potentially freeze the system into a lockstep that overlooks individual differences and the stark reality of a world that will simply not stand still, not for a minute. Few, if any, tests measure the full range of talents and abilities. Much of what we'll need to know and be able to do in the future may not even show up on our radar, because we'll have to invent it. (p. 289)

The lack of balance in our current system has frozen public education in place. While many education agencies and administrators push for individualized learning, differentiated instruction (both in pacing and delivery), or flipped classrooms, the success of these approaches is still measured by a single score derived from a multiple-choice test given on one day. As long as this is our primary tool for measuring success, all the creative and personalized approaches will be stifled. We propose a container model of accountability as a means of fostering personalization rather than stifling it.

The purpose of accountability is to ensure that schools are doing their jobs and meeting the needs of students. In other words, educational assessments should measure what students are learning and how they are progressing. The structure we propose for doing this in a comprehensive, holistic manner focused on personalized growth stems from a model for talk therapy.

Dr. John L. Garcia (1996) lays out a model for promoting positive growth and change in a therapeutic setting: the helping crucible. While education is not therapy, the two professions do share an overlapping goal: promoting positive growth and change for the individual. The model of the helping crucible can readily be adapted and applied to education.

In our lead-in story we compared our current system with a pressure cooker. The education crucible we are proposing is a very different container than a pressure cooker, although we will stick with the cooking analogy to continue to whet your appetite. A crucible is a pot used for melting. In the education crucible, the structure is created by the curriculum, the school calendar, the classroom, the school day, and the teacher.

These structures create an environment for learning that allows flexibility within the defined parameters. The teacher is no longer placed in the position of giver of knowledge; rather the teacher is the facilitator and modulator of the student's learning. The teacher modulates the intensity of the heat for each student to help foster the growth and change.

To stick with our cooking metaphor, think of boiling an egg. The teacher ensures the water doesn't boil over and ensures that the egg isn't undercooked. Likewise, the teacher can modulate the boiling to produce a soft-boiled or hard-boiled egg depending on the preferred outcome. This is quite unlike the pressure cooker, which can't be so easily regulated, and instead produces only intense heat and a more standard outcome.

Within this structured container, the freedom for personalization can be realized. Student learning can be measured when the student is ready, rather than at a predetermined time. A container model of accountability will measure the positive growth and change among individual students and hold teachers and schools accountable based upon a more value-added approach. This will foster and reinforce more of the differentiation and individualization that is already occurring. The accountability container will also infuse another counseling element: play therapy.

In her book *What Happened to Recess and Why Are Our Children Struggling in Kindergarten*, Susan Ohanian (2002) highlighted the real-life casualties of the increasing emphasis of standardized testing. Sadly, over a decade later, things have only worsened. As we discussed in chapter 2, play is the brain's natural milieu for learning. All mammals engage in it. The human brain has evolved to learn in this manner.

Given the overwhelming research that supports the use of play in brain development and learning, one would think that this method would be very prevalent in schools. Yet, the opposite is true, not only does our current school model take all the play out of learning—it takes away play time to focus more on standardized learning. In doing so, we've actually made our jobs even harder. The current accountability model forces our students to a more passive role—listening and regurgitating; hunting for what someone else deems to be the right answer instead of creating and generating their own solutions.

The education crucible calls for infusing more play into school. It integrates the play therapy model with the schooling. In play therapy, there is a structured environment with an intentional selection of toys. Within the structure, the child is allowed freedom and creativity and is guided in his or her growth by the active facilitation of the therapist. Incorporating aspects of this model will increase the child's learning and participation. Rather than focusing on the skill of passive listening, infusing elements of play into the education crucible will help the student develop mastery, autonomy, and ownership.

This crucible creates an environment that is more brain-mind compatible and fosters an experience that Dewey emphasized in his pedagogic creed over one hundred years ago, "that education must be conceived as a continuing reconstruction of experience; that the process and the goal of education are one and the same thing" (Dworkin, 1959, p. 27).

The Case for Standardized Testing

> If an exam effectively gauges a student's mastery of U.S. history or English grammar, then teaching the test is simply a matter of helping students develop that knowledge. Teachers who feel that a test ignores something essential should commit to fixing the test, not condemning the entire practice of testing. (Augustine, 2013)

Augustine is countering the argument that standardized testing forces teachers to teach to the test. His argument holds logic. The purpose of an exam is to measure. Just as a medical exam assesses one's health, an academic exam should measure one's knowledge. As teachers ourselves, we often face the ubiquitous complaining about exams by students. "Why do we have to take a test?" A simple explanation for this lies in a metaphor. If we wanted to know how tall our students were, we could do that with a measuring stick.

Because we couldn't put a ruler up to their brain to measure what they had learned, we had to give them a test. We hoped that our teacher-made tests were valid and reliable. Perhaps the future holds a technologically advanced measuring stick for the human brain—a simple way to visually see if our students have absorbed the knowledge and information we intend. Until then, we rely on more indirect methods. Standardized tests do help ensure better reliability and validity than teacher-made tests. Yet, how well do they measure progress toward fulfilling the two ultimate goals for learning: survival and a deeper understanding of the abstract?

The logic of Augustine's assertion hinges on the supposition that standardized tests do, indeed, measure progress toward the first goal for learning. Yet, that is a huge unknown in the long term. Indeed, research tends to indicate that grades are a better predictor of future success than test scores. Moreover, the question is: do standardized tests accurately measure a student's proclivity to succeed in life—which is what we are preparing them for (work, citizenry, etc.)?

Preparing Students for the Ultimate Test: Life

When a coach is preparing his or her team for competition, does he or she give the team standardized tests to see if they are ready for the big game? Absolutely not! The game is the test and the coach prepares them in many ways: skill drills, practice, film, and studying plays. Standardized tests can be part of the equation with accountability. The fallacy is that they are the be-all, end-all measure of effective learning and teaching.

That simply is not true. If we really want to measure learning and truly hold schools accountable then we need to be willing to do it right and not settle for a cheap sound bite. Going back to the medical analogy, a doctor doesn't judge your health based on a multiple-choice test. The doctor also doesn't simply take your temperature and judge your health on that. When you get a physical, you get multiple measures: temperature, blood pressure, blood samples, cholesterol, eyes, heart rate.

The recent push to assign schools a letter grade is not a bad idea. How we get to that grade is vital. It needs to be akin to a medical evaluation. Standardized test scores can be part of that evaluation, that equation; but currently it is the sole measure, and that is not effective or accurate. Does anybody want to be the best butter-churner? We don't need to compete with China, Singapore, or South Korea on test scores. Standardization is the past. The container model is the future, and the future is now.

References

Augustine, N.R. (2013, August 1). High marks for standardized tests. *The Washington Post*. Retrieved from https://www.washingtonpost.com/opinions/high-marks-for-standardized-tests/2013/08/01/34947a2a-eb4f-11e2-a301-ea5a8116d211_story.html

Dworkin, M. (1959). *Dewey on education*. New York, NY: Teachers College Press.

Fite, K. E., & Garcia, J. L. (2006/2007). A perspective on ritual: Toward a direction for revitalizing learning communities. *Journal of Creativity in Mental Health, 2*(1). doi:10.1300/J456v02n01_07

Garcia, J. L. (1996). *Personal workbook to accompany the professional counselor: A process guide to helping* (third edition). Boston, MA: Allyn and Bacon.

Marx, G. (2014). *21 trends for the 21st century: Out of the trenches and into the future*. Bethesda, MD: Education Week Press.

Ohanian, S. (2002). *What happened to recess and why are our children struggling in kindergarten?* New York, NY: McGraw-Hill.

Sirota, D. (2014, August 4). @davidsirota [Tweet] Retrieved from https://twitter.com/davidsirota/status/496312297011175424

Vollmer, J. (2010). *Schools cannot do it alone*. Fairfield, IA: Enlightenment Press.

5
Overcoming Pedagogical Paralysis[1]

> Although the term paradigm crisis may be evocative of something radical or transformational, the assumption here is that there can be nothing more critical than sharing with all children in all schools what the field knows about better ways to teach and learn. Not to do so is to deny those children the maximum opportunity for moral, economic, and social health and well-being, all of which are inextricably connected to the quality of the education that they receive.
>
> —Alan Bain, *The Self-Organizing School*

Recently, Dr. Phil McGraw of the *Dr. Phil* television program featured two parents who have chosen what they call "radical unschooling." Unschooling is an arm of the homeschool movement. Where homeschooling embraces the idea that children learn better and faster in the home environment, unschooling takes that to the next level by dictating that children learn better and faster on their own without the structure of formalized curriculum or time tables.

The father of the family featured on the program talked about the bad experience he had in traditional school. As a result, he along with his wife vowed that their four children would prepare for life by learning completely self-directed so that novelty and curiosity would drive their internal motivation, thus resulting in learning being fun, desired, and lifelong. The father went on to say, what many other parents have said, that traditional school was not relevant to most learners and as long as it wasn't relevant, students would not be intrinsically interested. The process or methods of learning are simply not centered on the learner.

Of all the things that may have changed in schools over the past 150 years, many would argue that the methods of instruction, while they have changed some, are the area of the least change in American public education. Ongoing research, conducted since the inception of teacher preparation programs, clearly indicates that a significant number of teachers, perhaps even a majority, teach the way they were taught as students and not in accordance with their training.

In other words, a student going through grade school, high school, and college is much more likely to then teach their students in the same manner they were taught all those years than any alternate way in which they were trained during their two- to three-year teacher preparation program. Couple this difficulty in overcoming the years of their actual education experience with the pressure of high-stakes testing and under this stress, our teachers regress. The pressure cooker we described in chapter 4 yields a fight, flight, or freeze response.

When our teachers freeze and take solace in teaching the way that they know—not the way that they were trained—this creates what we characterize as a *pedagogical paralysis*. With this paralysis, the educator is unlikely to alter or change his or her methods of teaching despite advances made in instructional techniques or in the individual discipline itself. Amazing and far-reaching advances in the neurosciences are one such example worthy of discussion if public education is to return to greatness.

Active Ignorance

Since the late 1960s, when neuroscience was in its infancy, the field has made substantial and significant advances in major areas: (a) in our understanding of how the brain works, and (b) in the technology available to gain, measure, and broaden that understanding. What is incredibly puzzling is that these advances have been slow to make their way into public education in the United States even though many of those advances have positively affected education in other developed countries. Caine and Caine (2001) argue:

> that ultimately, the key to really effective education is to align the best of what is known about learning and teaching with systems that facilitate such learning and teaching, appropriately supported by the larger within which education occurs. The alignment may, but will not necessarily, occur in the United States. However there is absolutely no doubt that those communities that grasp and implement such an alignment will develop a vastly superior system of education, and in the medium to long-term they will clearly have a significant competitive edge. (p. vi)

To be sure, because the field is relatively young, pediatricians, neuroscientists, and educators alike have not always agreed on the implications of what has been learned. Left brain versus right brain dominance is just one such example of controversy, and further research should be done so that common ground can be identified.

However, there is much that is agreed upon, particularly in the areas of cognitive processing and memory that has also been slow to permeate American educators' practice. Even worse, bits and pieces of things learned, out of context, have found their way into the conversation, which has resulted in confusion and controversy within some advances in the neurosciences that if correctly understood would be critical and relevant information for educator practice.

Traditional schools were and generally still are grounded in behaviorist theory, more specifically the Pavlovian thought of conditioned response. Pavlov demonstrated that a dog could be conditioned to drool just as it would upon seeing red meat. By ringing a bell each time the subject dog saw the red meat and began drooling, over time the dog becomes "conditioned" and eventually will drool with only the introduction of the bell.

Many methods of instruction used in traditional education are grounded in this theory and "conditioned response" remains, arguably, the dominant behaviorist understanding affecting instruction in schools today in the United States. In our complex adaptive world, that theory seems a bit bizarre given what we know about the brain and learning today, yet educational practice has seemingly not changed away from it.

Neuroscience and advances made in that field have yielded another line of thinking known as cognitive science theory and brain-compatible instructional theory. These critical advances largely reject conditioned response; and the more we learn about the brain, the stronger these advances seem to reject it. Once believed the two lines of thinking could peacefully coexist within the same educator and classroom, time seems to demonstrate the two lines of thinking are generally mutually exclusive and thus the controversy strengthens.

Memorization is one form of conditioned response. While a neuroscience grounded educator acknowledges there are occasions when memorizing is useful, that acknowledgment further realizes it is greatly limited and usually very inefficient. Additionally, memorization does not promote critical thinking or deep understanding of the content and can only be a means to some other ends for learning to authentically occur and that learning to penetrate the learner's long-term memory. Memorization is simple and prevents the mind to critically process the information and seek deep meaning.

Traditional pedagogy in the United States largely ignores much of the advances in neuroscience, and American student performance is suffering. Traditional pedagogy is generally simple and was useful in a former time—an industrial time that, too, was much simpler than the complex times of today.

Complexity

Complexity theory explains so much about what is both right and wrong with modern pedagogy. Right in its attempt to be natural, but wrong in its lack of acknowledgment of the complexity of both the brain and of the complex system that is the learner's world and environment. Not all learning, and little meaningful learning, can be reduced to a few simple facts or concepts.

To understand complexity theory and today's world, you have to look back to the frame of reference that has informed our understanding for centuries. That understanding comes from Descartes and Newton who thought and wrote before the emergence of the atomic age. With the coming of the atomic age, scientists, through force of facts, began calling into question the very basic understandings and writings of Descartes and Newton (Capra, 1984).

Cartesian and Newtonian accounts of the world were almost exclusively mechanistic and linear. The atomic age produced an understanding that was far more dynamic, which creates great conflict in grappling with centuries old understandings. However, these conflicts provided an enormous opportunity—and opportunity for those scientists to seek new and deeper meaning by constructing new forms, language, and concepts that would attempt to acknowledge the newly discovered phenomenon.

Complexity theory was a natural byproduct of systems theory, which defined an interconnected system made up of many parts (an evolution of Descartes theory of matter). Complexity then explains this interconnectedness by exploring the relationship of the parts with one another and the relationship the parts individually and collectively have with the system as well; hence, a dynamic relationship as opposed to our traditional mechanistic understanding stipulated by Cartesian thinking.

Complexity was critical for understanding systems since cybernetics came from the study of mathematics and physics (quantum mechanics) and was thus completely understood using equations and math. Complexity theory applies equally to both physical and social systems and relies on more than just mathematics as proof—a phenomenon referred to as the *new sciences*.

The new sciences remarkably explores our multiple, complex, adaptive systems network into larger systems. Interestingly, this new found perspective is evident in many schools in what is called the professional learning community (PLC). However, while this postmodern application of the new sciences has affected how some schools organizationally attempt to function, it largely has *not* affected how classrooms function or how pedagogy facilitates learning in those classrooms.

The PLC, as a model of organizational development, is a great acknowledgment of the new sciences, but this understanding must also permeate the classroom and how students engage learning. To do so will result in development of the individual child as opposed to the standardized child. Individual development happens naturally through self-organization; all living things self-organize. Complexity explains the interconnection of living things through the self-organization of those living things.

The underpinnings of the PLC rely on the learning community adapting and changing through the self-organization of the living things within the learning community. As you frame this concept, try to imagine how a classroom would look and feel if all children were expected and allowed to function and engage in a naturally self-organizing classroom.

Self-Organization

The Handbook of Educational Theories (2013) explains that living things self-organize by self-maintaining, self-renewing, and self-transcending:

Self-Maintaining

Although dependent on their environment, living things are not determined by their environment as evidenced by naturally maintaining themselves. Animals, including human beings for example, have a natural sense of urgency when threatened that continues until the threat is neutralized or alleviated. The more sophisticated the animal, the more options and tools available. The body of living organisms regulates the supply of a variety of things such as vitamins, hormones, and oxygen as the body increases or decreases the demand for the same. Plants self-maintain in their search for light and water that result in growth toward those resources (foliage for light and roots for water) in order to insure an adequate supply. (Jones, 2013, p. 808)

Self-Renewing

Living things constantly renew themselves. For example, a body of a blood donor will replace the blood taken from the body in less than eight weeks. That same body replenished most of the cells of the pancreas in less than twenty-four hours. The most obvious example of self-renewing may be in the loss of thousands of skin cells every minute, yet we never lose our generally same appearance as our bodies replace those cells and maintain a similar pattern of organization. A lizard losing its tail will grow a new one in order to continue to store necessary fat and other nutrients. The lizards' built-in tourniquet in the base of the tail is designed to easily constrict to prevent significant blood loss until the tail replaces itself with new growth. This cycle will only occur two or three times as if the lizard remembers losing it before and as part of self-maintenance determines it is unneeded or undesirable. (p. 808)

Self-Transcending

Finally, and perhaps most interestingly, living things self-transcend. Living things have an inherent tendency to adapt and change as needed. In the process of adapting, changing, or transcending, living things become very creative (to deal or cope with the adaptation or change) which then fuels new forms and ideas. The human brain, for example, naturally conceptualizes and analyzes anything it encounters or contemplates. Self-transcendence is what makes humans constant and natural learners; learning that can only be turned off when the body ceases to function or dies. Further, its activity is enhanced by novelty and curiosity and thus intrinsically motivated making the transcendence natural and unavoidable. In education, students may not be motivated to learn a particular lesson on a particular day, but that does not mean they are not motivated to learn. Learning is transcendence and thus is as natural as eating or breathing. (p. 808)

Voices from the Field

Instructional Leadership Transformation: A Natural Learning Perspective

As I prepared to create a plan with my leadership team to transform a low-performing school into a high-performing learning organization, I began to ponder the challenges of current teaching practices. The traditional answer was more interventions, more resources, higher expectations, and ensuring we were teaching the curriculum with fidelity. With much blood, sweat, and tears, this approach could probably fix the low scores temporarily, but would it be a sustainable transformation? Therefore, we began to dig deeper into the reasons behind our challenges.

After examining our current practices, we discovered that our teachers had a passion for their students. They wanted them to succeed. They worked long hours already and couldn't give much more **time** *to their work. We needed to begin to work smarter, not harder, to help our children succeed. So, we needed to dig deeper into our instructional practices to determine the root cause of why our teaching wasn't transitioning to long-term retention of the learning.*

We discovered a few common themes of traditional instructional approaches. First, as we all know, we tend to teach our students in the way that we were taught and by the process of how we learn. We noticed that traditional instructional implementation was the result of the experiences of the teacher or a singular instructional approach provided by a textbook or other resource. Instructional activities are provided by the teacher and only offered a single application of the learning to the students. Although this method works for some students, others are still left with gaps in the learning objectives.

Second, we discovered that teachers spend the majority of their time planning for interventions because the students were not learning the content the first time. Time is a precious commodity to educators, and we tend to spend the majority of our time preparing for what to do when the student doesn't learn. Preparation time for classroom instruction is, therefore, minimal and topic driven.

Last, we recognized that many teachers believe that students learn because they were taught. Teachers work extremely hard to develop innovative approaches to lesson design, integrating technology, and providing hands-on activities to engage the learners; however, achieve-

ment scores across the nation support that the learning is not sticking for all students. Teachers are using the tools that they were provided by our higher education preparation programs, their experiences in school, and their ongoing professional learning opportunities. They do a great job of using the tools that we, as instructional leaders, provide for them. Therefore, the challenge for instructional leaders is how to begin to transform our traditional approaches to teaching into a system that supports learning for all students?

Leading a transformation of this kind requires the nerve and willingness to take risks based on what is best for our students. Our leadership team had to first commit to understanding that our students come first and this would not be an easy transformation. Then, we had to begin the process of educating our staff on how the brain works and learning occurs. We had to create a paradigm shift in their minds that learning was a product of the experiences of each child and not the prospective of the teacher. They had to come to an understanding that short-term retention of knowledge was not our goal and student success was based upon finding a way to ensure learning was sustained. The initial professional development and paradigm shift in their thinking was instrumental before change could begin.

Once the staff began to understand the implications on continuing our traditional approaches to learning and the need to transform our instructional approach, we had to provide focused professional learning and collaborative planning time for teachers and instructional leaders. This time to work and plan together was the most important aspect to transforming our staff into brain-based instructors. The time was created on a daily basis for teachers and administrators to collaborate through a structured planning process. The administrator presence each day showed commitment to the cause and allowed for continued growth and accountability to reach our goals.

During the planning process, our teams focused on designing learning opportunities that structured their classrooms to allow for daily brain-compatible and natural learning instructional strategies such as planning activities in short segments, transitioning by walking to another seat in partner pair-share, creating competitive formative assessments, and so on. We focused on "beginning at the end" and allowing the students to create their own pathway and processes for the learning instead of slowly building foundational skills and until we reached the

(continued)

> *rigor of the learning objective. Our activities were designed to allow students multiple entry points into problem solving to encourage a connection with their own past experiences. We made time for at least one multiday group project per instructional unit to allow students to present their problem solving to their peers. And, we implemented questioning procedures in class that forced teachers to make students struggle to the point of cognitive conflict until the student discovered the answer—this took a little parent training.*
>
> *The result at the end of our first year was a sustainable transformation into a learning-focused campus that helped improve our school from a state-identified low-performing school into a top-performing school in our district and state. However, this transformation is not about test scores; it is about learning and meeting the needs of the individual student. It means individualization and not standardization! Instructional transformation begins with leadership and the willingness to be bold in our efforts to do what we know is right for students and their futures.*
>
> —Dr. Justin Terry, Forney Independent School District, Forney, Texas

To help teachers and administrators apply this new vision of schools, pedagogy, and learning, Caine and Caine (1997) summarize these concepts as follows:

> [We discuss] the changes in our collective philosophy as the new sciences, systems thinking, and comparable developments in other fields come to replace a Newtonian frame of reference. We introduce the new paradigm from the perspective of several new developments, the core of which is *complexity theory*. We explore ways in which complex adaptive systems self-organize. We suggest that the central issue with education is that, although the system is becoming more dynamical and is moving toward the edge of possibility, the fundamental ideas and purposes of traditional approaches to education still inhibit the appropriate type of change and adaption. The new paradigm requires a new type of person. The key to the emergence of that person—the possible human—is to better understand what human potential means in terms of brain research and other developments, and then to teach to actualize that potential. (p. ix)

Self-organization, by its very nature, creates a rippling and displacing effect as living things adapt and change. New information creates turbulence to the system and the living things it contains. Once living things' adaptation ripples and displaces other living things causes their adaption and changing through their own self-organization. This rippling or turbulence, often caused by new information, is how change occurs. Learning is adapting and changing—thus learning is change. Turbulence causes learning in a natural system. *The Handbook of Educational Theories* (2013) summarizes:

> In other words, one person's self-organization forces the self-organization of other living things in the system which, in turn, displaces back on the first person. In the quantum world (the concept was developed by a mathematician) that displacement is called *chaos* because it involves so much complicated information as opposed to a misunderstood definition of being devoid of order. Hence, the living system that we know as the universe is full of constant displacement and chaos making life itself interconnected. In education the concept has also benefitted with the advent of brain research. In the "brain world," displacement and chaos are called disequilibrium. (p. 808)

Disequilibrium and the Creativity It Causes

Disequilibrium, sometimes referred to as chaos, is a critical component of the new sciences and understanding complexity. Merriam-Webster Dictionary defines equilibrium first as "a state of intellectual or emotional balance" and "a state of adjustment between opposing or divergent influences or elements." The definition is further explained as a:

> state of balance between opposing forces or actions that is either static (as in a body acted on by forces whose resultant is zero) or dynamic (as in a reversible chemical reaction when the rates of reaction in both directions are equal).

If equilibrium is a state of balance, then disequilibrium is a state of imbalance. Scientifically speaking, if an object is in a state of balance then its velocity will stay constant. Thus, an object at rest will stay motionless if the forces are balanced. If an object is moving, then it will continue its trajectory at a constant velocity. But this is only if forces remain balanced, and in reality there are many unbalanced forces at play. We don't live in a vacuum, thus the world is typically in a state of disequilibrium—it is in constant motion and constant adaptation.

Think again of that vast, complex adaptive system. Self-organization of one living thing causes disequilibrium to other living things in the system as well as the system itself, thus causing more disequilibrium back on the system and so forth. My adaptation causes disequilibrium onto you and your resulting response causes the same back onto me and the other living things around you. Capra (1997) calls that the web of life; nothing in the web can move or change without impacting the web itself or the other vortexes of the web.

But do not despair all of this disequilibrium because complexity theory demonstrates that as the living things in the system self-transcend, they naturally adapt to the disequilibrium in the system or the web. But how, specifically? It's simple when you think about it and use another very natural trait in living things—creativity!

We naturally adapt to the messes and disequilibrium of our world by using our ability to be creative. The bigger the mess or the more chaotic the circumstance that confronts us, the greater the need we have for change and, therefore, the more reason we have to be creative so that we can drive our adaptation to the mess. Creativity is our natural response to the messes of life and the constant disequilibrium in which we live. It's as natural as breathing. Therefore, learning is as natural as breathing!

Natural Learning

Making learning natural? It seems simple, yet we have created schools that are actually very unnatural! Natural learning is all about allowing children to learn in a way that is completely natural to them. It is learning the way the brain and body naturally work as opposed to forcing learning in a way that is unnatural of inefficient to how that brain and body work. Natural learning is orderly but not controlled, as living things are not naturally controlled.

In fact, the more we are controlled, the more our brain resources will concentrate on not being controlled. If I want a learner to use all of his or her brain resources on the learning activity I have planned for the day, I better utilize pedagogy that naturally allows that learner to use those resources on that task. The less natural the activity, the less brain resources concentrating on that task.

The good news for educators is that our brain is a complex, adaptive system itself and perfectly suited to thrive in a world of disequilibrium, turbulence, or any other result of self-organization. Hence, our brain in a natural setting is perfect to deal with mess and is constantly learning and adapting based on information introduced into the system. The advent of brain research and the multitude of advances in the neurosciences has demonstrated this, and the more we learn about the brain the more capacity we know it has for dealing with disequilibrium.

Disequalibrium is usually less predictable and so is natural learning. Teachers do not have to figure everything out in a natural learning environment and everything in school does not have to be predicted or expected. In fact, learners use more of their brain capacity with just the opposite. Think about how much time teachers spend trying to make learning and class time totally predictable? They normally control things so tightly for that to be so.

Instead of controlling events, consider an orderly classroom governed by Caine and Caine's (2013) twelve brain/mind principles for teachers and educators that have been constructed from complexity theory and the advances in the neurosciences and can easily be applied to a teacher's pedagogy:

1. All learning engages the physiology as the brain/mind is a complex adaptive system.
2. The brain/mind is social.
3. The search for meaning is innate.

4. The search for meaning occurs through patterning.
5. Emotions are critical to patterning.
6. The brain/mind processes parts and wholes simultaneously.
7. Learning involves both focused attention and peripheral perception.
8. Learning is both conscious and unconscious.
9. There are at least two approaches to memory.
10. Learning is developmental.
11. Complex learning is enhanced by challenge and inhibited by threat associated with helplessness and fatigue.
12. Each brain is uniquely organized. (pp. 47–53)

These twelve principles have become the gold standard of the brain compatible learning movement. Principle ten, learning is developmental, is particularly critical in complexity as it indicates learning never stops and cannot be turned off. Thus, learning again is natural. Relevant learning, changing, and adapting are simply natural parts of living.

Teachers should never fool themselves that students are not motivated to learn. To the contrary, while they may not be motivated by a teacher's specific lesson or class, you cannot turn off their brain's natural learning just as you cannot turn off the body's natural breathing. The brain naturally learns anything it deems important, needed, or relevant.

In fact, the human brain is designed and naturally functions to deal with a world of mess, or disequilibrium, as Caine and Caine suggest in principals one, seven, and eight. Teachers are caring and compassionate people. To a fault sometimes, they attempt to make things so simple and predictable that they deny the learners an opportunity to utilize their natural creativity to find and seek solutions or answers.

In natural learning, the learner does not need the teachers to take things apart and put them back together. Our brain is constantly already doing that and the brain can do it for the individual learner much faster and more relevantly than someone else can do it for him or her. Oversimplification often prevents learning from penetrating the long-term memory because the brain never processes to the point of figuring out (cognitive conflict) where the new learning connects to prior learning and then fits into the individual's memory. Our brain needs to reconcile learning through this cognitive conflict to find the right place to store the information.

If the brain does not enter cognitive conflict, the mind will conclude the information is unneeded or irrelevant and with lightning fast speed discard the information. The same is true when the mind has unresolved conflicts with the new learning. Once the conflicts are resolved in the brain, the learner naturally locates the right and appropriate place to permanently store the new learning.

Cognitive conflict creates the requisite disequilibrium that is absolutely necessary for learning to occur and to be stored in long-term memory. In other words, it shakes things up! As Jones (2013) deepens the point:

> So true in fact, a brain that achieves equilibrium does not internally need to process, create, or construct but rather has reached a state of calm and no need. This phenomenon actually reduces brain activity. However, such equilibrium or state of calm, because of the dynamics of the complex adaptive system, physiologically never arrives until seemingly when the living thing dies. Death is the ultimate state of equilibrium in the quantum or complex world. Hence, although human beings often strive to achieve a state of equilibrium, to the brain that equilibrium never really happens. The complexity of the interconnections always provides some turbulence to the system and all living things within the system. Rather, the brain is constantly poised to deal with the next dose of chaos or turbulence that is sure to come as other living things self-organize around it. Once it does, the brain naturally becomes very creative in dealing with that mess as it made adaptations and constructed new forms and ideas necessary to transcend and self-organize as well. It takes the chaos, the turbulence, or the mess that is life to spur the brain into that creative stance. Self-transcendence, and thus new learning, depends on creativity.

> This is not to say that the more disequilibrium the better. In fact we have learned that ideally the brain needs a combination of stability and disequilibrium for total despair can lead

to downshifting of the brain (Caine & Caine, 1999; 2011). Likewise, a legitimate threat of health, safety or survival can hijack the brain to focus solely on that threat. So while disequilibrium is natural and a necessary part of self-transcendence, basic needs such as survival and safety must provide some degree of stability in order to avoid downshifting or for the brain devoting all of its resources to a threat or concern needing a higher priority. Complexity theory allows for this reality as complex systems can be dynamic and also be stable. Optimally, disequilibrium that exists in a safe or threat-free environment for the brain results in a state called relaxed alertness (Caine & Caine, 1999). Relaxed alertness is particularly optimal in learners in an educational setting. (Jones 2013, p. 809)

Shaken, Not Stirred

It is important to have the right amount of ebb and flow with this fluctuation between equilibrium and disequilibrium. Too much of either can lead to despair, learned helplessness, or a downshifting of the brain (Caine & Caine, 1999; 2011). It is vital for this natural learning to occur in a direction in a safe and nurturing environment as we discuss in chapter 7. The container model we have described in chapter 4 creates a structure wherein this dynamic and chaotic fluidity can occur in a direction that is guided by the educators. We want our students to be stimulated, but not overstimulated. We want our students to be calm, but not overly calm. The optimal educational setting fosters in our student a state of relaxed alertness (Caine & Caine, 1999; Jones 2013).

As said earlier, there is evidence of complexity in some schools and we do not suggest here that many schools have not had some evolution of ideas from the Cartesian and Newtonian roots to a more postmodern perspective. However, we are suggesting that teacher pedagogy in the United States has largely not evolved under the same thought.

Many U.S. teachers continue to uses methods and activities in the classroom that under brain-compatible and natural learning standards would be considered unnatural, linear, and lacking the dynamic nature of the real world we hope to prepare learners to thrive in. Traditional instruction, as we know it, does not reflect self-organization, which limits student's use of the brain's incredible and unique capacity.

Natural learning classrooms are more individualized and less standardized. They attempt to realize each learner's individual potential. Hence, pedagogy in a natural classroom is also more individualized and not standardized. Instead of teaching students the way they were taught in school, natural learning teachers have a plethora of instructional methods and pedagogy to cater learning.

While students in schools are expected to master a standardized curriculum, there should be very little standard in developing their individual potential. Curriculum may be standard as a matter of public policy and accountability but instruction (pedagogy) must be individualized per the needs of the learner. Self-organization is the epitome of a classroom that focuses on being learner-centered. Standardized instruction is counterproductive of being learner-centered.

While the principals of natural learning, complexity, and self-organization may be generally new to American education, they are not new to science and not new to many of the competing countries of the world. To overcome the pedagogical paralysis in American schools so that they can return to greatness, teachers and administrators must become more knowledgeable and sophisticated with neuroscience, brain research, and teaching to the individual student's potential. Only then will American schools become more individualized and learner-centered and less standardized.

Note

1. Elements of this chapter have been taken from the first author's work *Education for the Human Brain* and the chapter on Complexity Theory in *The Handbook of Educational Theories*, both of which have been clearly cited herein. As these are the primary sources for these major concepts in the knowledge base and in the case of the second work has been peer-reviewed, this method of presentation was selected to incorporate those ideas into the larger context presented in this chapter.

References

Bain, A. (2007). *The self-organizing school: Next-generation comprehensive school reforms.* Lanham, MD: Rowman & Littlefield.

Caine, R. N., & Caine, G. (1997). *Education on the edge of possibility.* Alexandria, VA: Association for Supervision and Curriculum Development.

Caine, G., & Caine, R. (2001). *The brain, education, and the competitive edge.* Lanham, MD: Scarecrow Press.

Caine, R. N., & Caine, G. (2011). *Natural learning for a connected world: Education, technology, and the human brain.* New York, NY: Teachers College Press.

Caine, R. N., & Caine, G. (2013). The brain/mind principles of natural learning. In T. Jones (Ed.), *Education for the human brain: A road map to natural learning in schools* (pp. 43–62). Lanham, MD: Rowman and Littlefield.

Capra, F. (1984). *The turning point: Science, society and the rising culture.* New York, NY: Bantam Books.

Capra, F. (1997). *The web of life: A new scientific understanding of living systems.* New York, NY: Anchor Books.

Equilibrium (n.d.). In *Merriam-Webster's online dictionary.* Retrieved from http://www.merriam-webster.com/dictionary/equilibrium?show=0&t=1294170292

Jones, T. B. (2013). Complexity theory. In G. Brown, B. Irby, and R. Lara-Alecio (Eds.), *Handbook of educational theories* (pp. 807–11). Charlotte, NC: Information Age Publishing.

Jones, T. B. (2013). *Education for the human brain: A road map to natural learning in schools.* Lanham, MD: Rowman and Littlefield.

6
Authentic Leadership

> And only well-informed, warm-hearted people can teach others things they'll always remember and love. Computers and TV don't do that. A computer teaches a child what a computer can become. An educated human being teaches a child what a child can become.
> —Kurt Vonnegut, *If This Isn't Nice, What Is? Advice to the Young — Graduation Speeches*

The mission of our schools is to educate our young; to prepare the next generation to take over for us. We've discussed rather thoroughly what this will need to look like in this century and the urgent need to return to the greatness that American public education once knew. It will take a new style of leadership to guide us in the right direction. Simple management is not enough, nor will an authoritarian style meet the demands.

A return to greatness in education will call for holistic authentic leadership. "The challenge beset for the educational leaders of the present and the future is one that will require a bridging and blending of old and new paradigm . . . the modern ethical leader must create a paradigm blend" (Barrett, 2013, p. 41). That paradigm blend begins with authentic leadership.

So what does it mean to be an authentic education leader in the twenty-first century? Our goal in this chapter is to explore that concept and provide an authentic definition of what it is, why it is needed, and how it can be cultivated.

A Definition of Terms

In a good debate it is important to first define terms. Thus, for this exploration, we look to the words' meanings as a starting point. *The New Oxford American Dictionary* (2014) defines *authentic* as "Of undisputed origin; genuine." What then, is the definition of *leadership*? *The New Oxford American Dictionary* delineates six definitions for a leader, two are pertinent here: "1) The person who leads or commands a group, organization, or country; 4) A short strip of nonfunctioning material at each end of a reel of film or recording tape for connection to the spool." When we look at the designated leaders in our school system, how often does the latter definition seem more applicable than the former? What does it take to truly lead or command a learning organization?

By a simple synthesis of dictionary definitions, an authentic leader would be defined as a genuine authority who commands a group or organization. But what does that look like in practice? And what does it truly mean for a person to be authentic, let alone an authentic leader? Likewise, leadership is an ambiguous word in many ways. There are many types of leaders and different types are often needed for different groups or situations.

Indeed, volumes have been written on the subject and there are a host of seminars and webinars on the topic in many arenas, especially business. One can even earn a doctorate degree in education leadership. And, still, it is an abstract concept that can be elusive to strictly define. For the purpose of this chapter, we take the very basic dictionary definitions of authentic and leadership, and use them as a jumping off point to delve deeper into the type of leadership that is necessary to return our public schools to greatness.

From Abstract to Concrete

While the abstract concept of authentic leadership may be difficult to strictly define in words, it does contain a visceral quality—you know it when you see it (and feel it). Indeed, there are individuals in our daily lives who embody such characteristics. These are individuals we look to as leaders because of who they are, not necessarily because of the title they hold. Take a moment and reflect on who in your life meets this definition. For our purposes here, let's look at one real-life example from the world of sports, Tony Dungy.

In the world of professional sports, it is not uncommon to see an irate coach pacing the sidelines screaming at the players and the referees. Tony Dungy, the first African American coach to win the NFL Super Bowl, was not that type of leader. In fact, the mild-mannered Dungy is widely heralded as a man who achieved greatness without sacrificing his values. Tom Landry is a similar example from an earlier generation.

In an interview with ESPN, Brad Stevens, then the newly appointed head coach of the Boston Celtics, was asked about what coaches influenced him the most. He cited Tony Dungy specifically. Stevens elaborated why:

> When I got a chance to sit down with Coach Dungy he was the same guy everybody portrayed him to be. It wasn't a different story behind closed doors. He is authentic. He is a leader. He is not overly verbose or loud, but you can tell that everyday there is a purpose to what their organization is doing. (Goodman, 2013)

Further, Stevens stated that Tony Dungy was the model for what type of leader he wanted to be. Brad Stevens, former head coach at Butler University and current head coach of the NBA's Boston Celtics, himself may be also considered an authentic leader. Stevens took a small school to the pinnacle of college basketball two straight years in a row and was then recruited to coach one the nation's most storied basketball programs.

Despite only playing college basketball at a small Division III school and never playing in the NBA, Stevens has landed one of the most coveted positions in all of professional sports. His leadership style is largely responsible for these accomplishments. Much of his authority with his players lies in his own authenticity and in his growth mindset.

Authentic Is Real

One common trait between Tony Dungy and Brad Stevens is that they remain true to themselves and their values. They don't succeed in spite of this, but rather because of this. They are authentic, real. "Being real" or "keeping it real" is an oft-quoted ideal, and one that isn't that easy to adhere to. Therapist Toni Raiten-D'Antonio has found a simple, yet powerful solution to this. The answer she found lies in the children's story of *The Velveteen Rabbit*. Raiten-D'Antonio used this story as a guide to help herself and her clients become real.

In her book, *The Velveteen Principles: A Guide to Becoming Real* (2004), the author proffers twelve principles to help a person be real (authentic) in a world of superficial objects. These principles can be applied to educational leadership as well. Raiten-D'Antonio took a classic tale written in 1922 and found within it a timeless parable with "the subtle power to provoke our deepest desires and inspire reflection" (p. xii). To us, that is also what an authentic leader does for an organization and its people. That is also what authentic learning does for the teacher and student. The authentic leader will provoke and inspire greatness.

Ripples of Authenticity

We've emphasized the importance of authentic learning opportunities throughout this book. For our current system to recapture its greatness and unleash the potential of our greatest resources, our human resources, we will need courageous, authentic leadership. It stands to reason that for there to be authentic learning, there must be authentic teaching, which requires authentic leadership.

With all the forces outside our control in the world, the one thing we can control is ourselves. While it has become a bit cliché, Gandhi's quote, "Change begins with the individual," still rings true. Indeed, just as helpers must take care of themselves to be present and helpful to their clients (to those they serve), leaders must do the same.

We are not looking for a superman or superwoman, quite the contrary. The style of leadership we are calling for is more humble and more subtle than that. It is also not prepackaged or standardized. Authentic leadership will look different for every individual and every community. The underlying commonality is the palpable "realness," the ability of that individual to connect, relate, support, and inspire.

The authentic leader is honest and trustworthy. This may seem self-evident, yet how often do we read scandalous headlines in the news regarding unethical misdeeds of our leaders? Money scandals, cheating on standardized tests, sex abuse—all these things weaken the public trust in public education. Just as the definition states, authentic is genuine not false or fictitious; and that is where honesty comes in. Parents are trusting educators with their most valuable possession (for lack of a better word)—their children.

It is imperative that educational leaders be honest and forthright. They must do so when having those critical conversations. Educational staff (teachers, secretaries, etc.) are trusting their leaders with their careers and, increasingly, their lives. An honest, genuine, trustworthy (authentic) leader provides stability and safety, which allows for more creativity, dedication, and the like.

We spoke extensively about accountability in chapter 4. The authentic leader holds people accountable in a good way. Feedback and reprimand will be easier to swallow because it is more valid and it is more trusted (not just based on personal bias, politics, or favoritism). This is where authenticity can serve to keep the leader grounded, humbled, and focused.

Authenticity in the Virtual World

The authentic leader is needed to combat the zombie school culture that has been created. While legislatures set the what, leaders can set the how. Authentic leadership is what is needed for our return to greatness. The "real" world that so many people refer to is not, in actuality, real. It is manufactured. It is our collective daydream (Ruiz, 1997). We have to live in this world and we have to prepare our students for it and we don't have to perpetuate its myth.

With the ever-increasing ubiquity of online classes, computers, technology, drones, and robots, the need for human connection is even greater. No amount of technology can replace the human connection. Our biology demands it. Modern education demands a real person who can translate the technology and help the teacher and student apply it in their own life. The human leader can help make that learning real.

In an ever-increasingly noisy world, honesty and authenticity will stand out (Vaynerchuck, 2013). It will stand out because of relationships. It will triumph in the end just like the velveteen rabbit. The shiny new toys are like all the quick fixes and fly-by-night interventions. That is why authentic leadership is vital to test everything and retain what is good. The authentic leader must see through the false facades. Learning and life are all about connections. Authenticity builds stronger connections both in human relationship and in authentic learning.

The Authentic Container Model

Ron Paul (2013) recently wrote, "The most meaningful way to improve the world is to free up the creativity of individuals" (p. 23). To paraphrase, the most meaningful way to improve education is to free up the creativity of the school/the learning community/the organization. Contrary to Ron Paul's assertions, however, privatization is not the best way to achieve this. The container model for public education can achieve this, however.

The authentic leader will cultivate a container model for education. This container is not a rigid structure. Rather, it is a means of harnessing the natural powers of human growth and learning and unleashing them in a guided manner. The authentic leader is not a dictator who burdens down thoroughbred horses, turning them into pack mules. Neither is the leader an overly permissive leader who lets the stallions run amok. No, this leader harnesses these thoroughbreds and unleashes them in a purposeful direction.

Margaret Wheatley (2006) talks about this dynamic of leadership in the context of our new scientific understandings. She also details the four things all living systems do, two of which are pertinent here: self-renewal and transcendence. Existential psychologist Rollo May (1983) echoes this:

> Existing involves a continual emerging, in the sense of emergent evolution, a transcending of one's past and present in terms of the future. Thus, *transcendre*—literally "to climb over or beyond"—describes what every human being is engaged in doing every moment when he is not seriously ill or temporarily blocked by despair or anxiety. (p. 143)

Sadly, our educational system is seriously ill and many of its constituents are blocked by anxiety and despair. It is the role of the authentic leader to provide a salve and remove that anxiety and despair.

The Authentic Leader and the New Paradigm

As educational leaders we must focus on a two-pronged approach to education: (1) pass on knowledge essential for survival (in our current society) and (2) evoke learning that is more insightful and intuitive—akin to Plato's ultimate aim for education. Just as light exists as both a particle and a wave, the authentic leader is simultaneously the facilitator of both types of learning: survival and understanding.

Peter Senge et al. (2012) point out that the school principal or administrator becomes a fulcrum point in the organizational learning model—balancing needs of parents, teachers, central administration, community, legislature, and one's own drives or goals. With educators and schools being pulled in so many directions the need for authenticity is simultaneously more difficult and more important. Balancing energies—between two goals of education, between needs and wants of stakeholders—and remaining true to the mission is critical for our return to greatness.

Senge (2006) described this type of shift/blend as *metanoia*, which means a shift of mind. Even in 1975, Capra lamented the lack of such a shift despite emergence of new scientific findings, sadly that status quo largely remains:

> I believe the world-view implied by modern physics is inconsistent with our present society, which does not reflect the harmonious interrelatedness we observe in nature. To achieve such a state of dynamic balance, a radically different social and economic structure will be needed: a cultural revolution in the true sense of the word. The survival of our whole civilization may depend on whether we can bring about such a change. (p. 307)

Research in the world of quantum physics and even biology is revealing a greater interconnectedness among all living systems. Cartesian mechanism was purposeful in bringing us to this point, but the model breaks down (no pun intended) with findings at the subatomic level. It is a model that has run its course and must now be integrated into this new understanding. This will be difficult for many individuals and organizations as it is a worldview that is deeply entrenched in our way of knowing.

Being Authentic Is Creating a Shared Vision

To be a *real* leader is to act as more of a facilitator. A real leader will create a shared vision, rather than impose his or her vision on an organization. A real leader will remove the barriers that prevent the natural flow within the organization. The real leader will reshape the images of the traditional roles of students and teachers, of classrooms and schools. The real leader will need to lessen the barriers between schools and communities.

As Johnston (1984, p. 367) wrote, "We should see the walls of the school becoming more permeable." Schools should be seen more as community resource centers. The real leader will need to reconnect the fragments created by the mechanistic system of education.

The Authentic Instructional Leader

Brain-compatible learning is authentic learning. It builds real connections in the brain. It physically changes the brain. John Dewey (1916) knew it was authentic even before the brain research that now validates him. The authentic leader is not only an instructional leader, but a lead-learner. Gone are the days of the classroom teacher as the sole source of knowledge who imparts this wisdom upon the students. In this increasingly connected, information age, the teacher has become a facilitator of learning.

Likewise, the educational leader becomes a facilitator and models learning. Facilitate comes from the Latin *facil*, which means easy. Thus the authentic leader breaks down barriers to growth and learning and paves the way (makes easier) for self-renewal, growth, and learning for all encompassing the learning community. With the fast-paced changes happening in technology, it is difficult to keep up with everything.

The educational leader must champion the way for all to continuously learn and improve. This includes parents and the community. We should start to see parents as interdependent partners in the learning. We hold parent education classes about Internet safety, high school graduation requirements, and the like, and this must continue to grow. Authentic leaders will encourage parents to learn as well. It doesn't end with a diploma or degree but continues until we die. This is where walls become more permeable.

Many teachers fear that not knowing something will strip them of their authority and they are often afraid to admit they

Voices from the Field

It was never my goal to be an administrator. I certainly didn't set out to become an educational leader. What I wanted to do was be the most effective teacher I could be and to reach as many learners as possible as completely as I could. For goodness sake, I had a newly acquired house payment, a wife who was expecting, and a new car with a monthly payment—I just wanted a job doing something I loved! That's how it began.

As a new teacher I tried to employ many of the strategies and values I had witnessed as a student and I had only studied: treating human beings with respect, caring about students' well-being as much as their authentic learning, assisting learners to connect the dots between subject matters, drawing from all experiences, creating a sense of community where exploring was safe and mistakes were a necessary part of growth, and modeling how a learner learns.

It was later in my career that I realized I could affect more students by assuming a new position. The position of principal would offer me an opportunity to establish a climate and a shared drive to achieve throughout an entire school community. This would become my life's work.

Effective leadership requires all the attributes needed by a classroom teacher as well as management skills and, most importantly, communication skills. A personality trait that is often overlooked is a positive sense of humor. I have found that the inclusion of humor in most every aspect of teaching, leading, and living is an asset. We need to have the ability to laugh at ourselves!

We may be leaders, but we are not infallible and we certainly are not all-knowing. Mistakes happen and the strength is in recognizing errors and correcting them. Doing so with a sense of humor makes it all palatable.

Positive humor can also win over students and teachers, as well as parents and community members. It can defuse tense situations, lessen resistance, and create a sense of commonality. Good humor never belittles or embarrasses others. It causes smiles if not outright laughter. Progress is made when walls come down!

It is also important for authentic leaders to listen with their hearts. The position of principal opens many doors, not the least of which includes making students, teachers, parents, and community members understand that we are all human. Decisions that are life changing for others should never be coldhearted decisions. Empathy is key. Ask yourself, "If roles were reversed, how would I feel?" Place yourself in others' positions when making decisions and when choosing words.

It is imperative that leaders spend time in the classroom. Without that ongoing experience, any provided leadership becomes merely exercises in theory. What works on paper does not always do more than spin wheels in the classroom.

Working directly with students lends itself to maintaining a grounded approach as to what is needed from the leader. It also helps keep fresh the frustrations and difficulties that students and their teachers combat daily. Reading for ten minutes to a kindergarten class can certainly bring you back to reality. Leaders model good teaching.

Substitute for a teacher, guest lecture about topic you know, do lunch duty! Be in the classroom—it's that simple.

An important strategy to create a desirable fluid educational environment is the sincere inclusion of all stakeholders. Obviously, teachers and students must be at the center of a successful equation, but parents and community leaders need involvement as well. An authentic educational leader sets a welcoming atmosphere. Student learning must be at the core of decisions.

Faculty Cabinet needs to be a problem-solving committee, not just a sounding board for complaints. Parent-Teacher organizations should foster activities that bring familiarity between parents and teachers, not just raise monies for supplies and playground equipment. School Improvement Teams should work to alter situations that impede student learning, not just create rhetoric to publish or send to the central office or DOE. Operational rules and guidelines must be made with an understanding of the effect they will have.

Becoming an authentic educational leader is an ongoing endeavor. What worked yesterday might very well not work today and most likely will not work tomorrow. Authentic and effective leadership is elusive. Follow your training and your heart. Love the profession, care for the learners, and enjoy your calling.

—Gene Theriac, Retired Principal,
Evansville Vanderburgh School Corporation,
Evansville, Indiana

don't know something or admit a mistake. This is a mistaken concept; it is part of the fixed mindset (Dweck, 2006).

Likewise, many leaders are afraid to show ignorance because they fear appearing weak. This is a false façade. It likely served leaders well during the dark ages when we had less knowledge of the greater world, so a seemingly omniscient authority provided comfort and security and people blindly followed. In this era, that is no longer needed—it is impossible to be omniscient today. What we need today are leaders who are willing to learn, willing to question, and willing to grow.

Wheatley (2006) examined seeing organizations that are learning to use the power of self-organization to be more agile and effective. (Think of the Kodak story.) They have eliminated rigidity both physically and psychologically. They have knocked down walls and created workplaces where people, ideas, and information circulate freely. They have simplified roles into minimal categories. Finland does this with their national standards. They have them but they are written briefly. Not the intricate amassment of details like so many state standards. Finland's standards allow for creativity. The goal is the same, but the path may be different.

Our twenty-first-century authentic educational leader must have the courage to break down the ever-hardening walls of rigidity that are forming in our educational system. On June 12, 1987, standing at the Brandenburg Gate of the Berlin Wall, U.S. President Ronald Reagan decried "Mr. Gorbachev, tear down this wall!" We say now, "educational leaders, tear down these walls!"

References

Barrett, D.C. (2013). Holistic, ethical leadership for the 21st century. *School Leadership Review*, 8(2), 41–51.
Capra, F. (1975). *The Tao of physics: An exploration of the parallels between modern physics and eastern mysticism.* Boston: Shambala.
Dewey, J. (1916). *Democracy and education.* New York: Macmillan.

Dweck, C. S. (2006). *Mindset: The new psychology of success.* New York: Ballantine Books.
Goodman, J. (2013, October 23). Brad Stevens conversation. *ESPN Sportscenter Conversation.* Retrieved from http://espn.go.com/video/clip?id=9866661
Johnston, C. M. (1984). *The creative imperative: A four-dimensional theory of human growth and planetary evolution.* Berkeley, CA: Celestial Arts.
May, R. (1983). *The discovery of being.* New York: W. W. Norton.
New Oxford American Dictionary Online. (2014). *Authentic.* Retrieved from http://www.oxforddictionaries.com/us/definition/american_english/authentic
New Oxford American Dictionary Online. (2014). *Leader.* Retrieved from http://www.oxforddictionaries.com/us/definition/american_english/leader
Paul, R. (2013). *The school revolution: A new answer for our broken educational system.* New York, NY: Grand Central Publishing.
Raiten-D'Antonio, T. (2004). *The velveteen principles: A guide to becoming real.* Deerfield Beach, FL: Health Communications.
Ruiz, M. A. (1997). *The four agreements.* San Rafael, CA: Amber-Allen Publishing.
Senge, P. (2006). *The fifth discipline: The art and practice of the learning organization.* New York, NY: Doubleday.
Senge, P., Cambron-McCabe, N., Lucas, T., Smith, B., Dutton, J., & Kleiner, A. (2012). *Schools that learn: A fifth discipline fieldbook for educators, parents, and everyone who cares about education.* New York, NY: Crown Business.
Vaynerchuck, G. (2013). *Jab, jab, jab, right hook: How to tell your story in a noisy social world.* New York: HarperCollins.
Wheatley, M. J. (2006). *Leadership and the new science: Discovering order in a chaotic world,* 2nd ed. San Francisco, CA: Berrett-Koehler Publishers.

7
The Price of Safety

> Today I seek to do one thing that interrupts a pattern of fear. Today is the day of my release, as I declare myself free from the bondage of the ego. I will do one thing, however small, to forge a path of greatness where I have formerly cowered in fear. I need not repair every aspect of my wounded self today. Rather, I need only practice the thinking and behavior of a greater good. With this, I build new pathways in my brain and in my life.
>
> —Marianne Williamson, *A Year of Miracles*

April 20, 1999, is a date that lives in infamy in America. Americans were glued to their television sets as the events at Columbine High School in Littleton, Colorado, unfolded. Since then there have been many mass shootings, especially at schools: Sandy Hook, Virginia Tech, UC Santa Barbara (UCSB). Columbine wasn't the first and it wasn't the last.

Indeed, the odds are high that in the time since the date of the publication of this book and the point at which you are reading it there have been multiple mass shooting incidents in America—and quite likely one of those was at a school. No, tragically Columbine is not an anomaly, but it was a point of cultural shift.

It was by far the worst school shooting at the time and it was the first to be televised. In pre-9/11 America, this made it a turning point in the American psyche.

Sadly, these types of events are almost commonplace now. Columbine, however, was unique for its time and truly shocked our nation. While on a national scale such violent incidents as those that occurred at the Aurora Theater, UCSB, and Virginia Tech are becoming commonplace and numbing to the public at large, they are still very real to those who have lived through them and suffered losses of loved ones. Moreover, these incidents eat away at the psyche of our modern public school system. Even though the incidence of such events are low, there is a very real fear for parents, teachers, and staff. In other words, while the mathematical odds are very low, the fear is not.

Parents have an undercurrent of fear every day their children are in school. This fear is, of course, amped up heavily by the media, especially with the twenty-four-hour news cycles. Likewise, faculty and staff have that same undercurrent of fear for their own personal safety. Dr. John Garcia, retired counseling professor from Texas State University, purports that, "Under stress, we regress." This undercurrent of fear is not healthy for our educational system.

But school shootings aren't the only threat to our schools' learning environments. Bullying, drugs, fighting, natural disasters, and the safety of academic freedom also serve to undermine the capacity for student growth in our schools. This capacity is undermined for teachers and students alike. These fear factors, if you will, detract from the nurturing environment necessary for students to take risks and make mistakes and the same is true for educators.

Standardized testing constricts this environment too. Bullying constricts it too. The coercive model of current accountability constricts this. The safety of the classroom is under attack from all angles. For schools to return to greatness, they must alleviate these threats as much as possible. A container-model school does this.

The Challenge of the Safety Imperative for Educators

No present-day book on education can be complete without addressing the issue of safety. It is far too broad and complex a topic to fully explore in the context of this book. However, the safety imperative itself is another threat to public schools as it undermines public trust and creates fear. The perception that our public schools are not safe environments for our children has two serious consequences:

1. Parents look elsewhere for their children's education like private schools and homeschooling.
2. It detracts from the learning environment and, thus, undermines our schools' effectiveness. The real downfall of public education could be the issue of safety—not vouchers, charters, budget cuts, or high-stakes testing.

To remedy these threats will take a concerted, consistent, and calculated effort. This chapter will address the important aspects of safety and offer hope with the medicine that is a brain-compatible, holistic school.

The authentic leader we discussed in chapter 6 is faced with a major challenge today: creating a safe school in the face of budget constraints and mounting pressures from various factions. This safety imperative is of the utmost importance, however, for no authentic learning can occur without it. Similar to what we discussed regarding holistic accountability in chapter 4, schools deserve credit for all that they do to keep our children safe.

But even more important are the mundane examples of teachers and educators feeding children with own money; providing school supplies or clothing; helping them with personal grooming; and reporting incidents of abuse and neglect to CPS. Our schools do much to meet the very basic safety needs of our nation's children every day and every hour. They need more resources to do a better job. They also need the freedom to do their job.

Just as Maslow emphasized a hierarchy of needs, the same holds true for learning in our schools. We do a lot for this—free breakfast, free lunch, the school nurse, free spinal exams, and hearing and vision screenings. Schools have begun taking stronger precautions to safeguard against food allergies. To get that deeper level of critical thinking that we emphasize and desire, schools do much to provide for the physical and emotional safety of their students. And yet, it still seems to fall short.

The strains of poverty and violence and the hype of fear generated by the twenty-four-hour news cycle are detracting from the greatness that could be. Schools must be transformed to overcome these challenges in the best way possible. There are many factors outside of the educator's control. However, there are many factors within our control. It is upon these factors that we must focus. The container model of brain-compatible, natural learning offers an integrated solution that generates an overall safer and more productive learning environment. Within this container model several types of safety are addressed. These different categories of safety fall under two umbrellas: physical and emotional.

Physical Safety

Abraham Maslow's famous hierarchy of needs starts from the ground up. Public schools have taken this hierarchy to heart addressing an increasing amount of physical needs of students. As we have pointed out in earlier chapters, schools face an ever-increasing burden, an increasing responsibility on the part of public schools to meet the basic, nonacademic needs of students.

Sadly, rather than being lauded for our efforts—or at least given tacit recognition for these feats—educators face a dump and blame phenomenon. More and more is required of schools and they receive more and more blame for society's ills. In basic training, Army recruits are given tasks wherein they are intentionally set up to fail. This is part of the breaking down and rebuilding process of creating a soldier. This strategy works well for building soldiers, but not so well for building schools. Especially when there is no building-up phase.

Nevertheless, public schools maintain their focus. Ensuring the physical safety of their staff and students is of primary concern. We cannot have an effective learning environment, our learning crucible, without meeting this most basic of needs. For our purpose here we look at physical safety through two basic threats: threats from without and threats from within.

Threats from Without

The container model begins with establishing boundaries. The chicken egg is a very good example of a near perfect container (although with too much external pressure it can be cracked or broken). These boundaries—in the case of the chicken egg, the shell—establish a protective barrier against outside threats. A chicken embryo could never develop outside of its protective shell. It would be a mass of goo susceptible to disease, predators, dirt, and the elements of weather.

Similarly, our student learners will never develop without a protective shell. The protective barrier for our schools starts with the building itself. (Of course, how soon is this compromised with portable buildings? It seems as if as soon as a new school is opened, it is too small and portable buildings must be added—already contaminating the nice protective barrier of the school building itself.)

New designs are incorporating technology and utilizing new knowledge about brain-based learning environments. Our new schools must be designed to keep students and staff safe from the elements and safe from intruders, and elicit learning. To best elicit learning our schools must be designed to allow for effective traffic flow of humans, have effective lighting, color schemes, and so on. We must be intentional and purposeful in the design of our buildings.

But the barriers we establish for external safety aren't just physical. Our procedures, policies, and routines also establish security. From policies regarding picking up students and volunteer check-ins to entering the building, vigilance must be adhered to regarding these practices.

Natural Disasters

Fire drills and tornado drills are very commonplace and even entrenched in our national psyche. Think of movies featuring students pulling the fire alarm to get a chance to meet outside for a scheme, mischief, or romantic interlude.

Probably everyone reading this book has memories of fire alarms (planned or unplanned) and perhaps a funny accompanying story. These mundane exercises, however, were no accident of happenstance. They are part of a readiness effort and required by law. Some of you reading may even recall bomb drills—getting under the desks in case of a Soviet attack. A safe, effective school takes these drills seriously. They are an instance wherein 99 percent of the time they are unnecessary and may seem tiresome or disruptive, but that 1 percent of the time that they become necessary, they are vital.

As part of our return to greatness and our container model, the modern school is engineered for safety. The physical container that is the school establishes the setting and the tone for the environment. The design is intentional and creates a flow and mood. A major part of that engineering and design is safety from natural disasters.

Modern buildings look quite different from their ancestors. As we continue to redesign our buildings to better facilitate this new learning environment, considerations for structural safety, as well as traffic flow must be taken into design.

Gun Violence

What is the psychology of attacking a school? Experts say the rate of school shootings is statistically unchanged since the mid- to late-1990s, yet it still remains a troubling burden on our collective minds. We referenced Columbine at the beginning of this chapter; that attack changed things in a psychological way. Similarly, Newtown, Connecticut, shifted things again as this was an attack from an outside threat and without warning. As we'll discuss shortly, the threats from within provide for a bit more control for educators.

Attacks from without, like Newtown, are harder to control. This is where the container is very important—the design of the building, the policies, procedures, routines come in to play. To return our schools to greatness, they must be safe. We are protecting our most cherished resource, our children, and therein our future, our collective progeny.

Our twenty-first-century school will have to balance this need. How do we design a school that is safe from the statistically unlikely, yet very real, Newtown-esque attack and doesn't resemble a prison? The solution to events of mass shootings, for example, is one that lies outside educators' hands. Meanwhile, as the debate rages on over the causes of and solutions to such events, schools have to find a way to keep their people safe. Another important thing is that we keep things in perspective.

For education leaders, there will be a balance struck—managing perceptions, that is countering fears hyped by media; plus ensuring parents, students, and staff feel safe and secure. Just as fire drills became routine and even mundane, but necessary, similar steps to ensure safety are important.

The twenty-first-century leader will also guard against going through the motions and will, instead, transform this into opportunities for empowerment. Having a plan with concrete steps and guidelines will help create the safe environment needed to promote growth. Educators must take the power back from the fear-mongers and transform it into empowerment for our schools and communities.

Threats from Within

The container model creates a boundary that protects from threats outside, but there are many threats to our learning environment from the inside. These pathogens must be addressed through preventive measures and through antibodies. This isn't a new thing, either. Schools have been addressing these internal issues for centuries. The scale of certain threats and the exacerbation through technology has changed things, however.

Voices from the Field

I have been a police officer for more than thirteen years and a majority of that time has been spent as a School Resource Officer (SRO) in the Texas Public School System. As an SRO, my job is to provide a safe learning environment for the students and a safe working environment for the staff. As the years pass, the future brings new safety problems that affect the success of today's schools. The SRO and school staff no longer just deal with an occasional, typical juvenile fight. Now, they must contend with active shooters, students assaulting teachers, bullying, guns, drugs, and gangs.

Through the many years working in schools and dealing with juveniles, the one major thing I have seen as a steady growing problem at all grade levels is the lack of accountability for juveniles for wrongdoing. When there is a lack of accountability, whether from parenting, educational law, or just the fear of being fired or sued, it tends to promote a certain amount of entitlement for juveniles. The entitlement and lack of discipline have created a fearless juvenile who is not afraid to cross the line and endanger himself or herself or others.

For today's average inner-city juvenile, the school should be a safe haven and a place of structure and social interaction, because at home it can be quite the opposite. With the promotion of violence in today's media (television, radio, movies, and video games), there is no question that media has created juveniles who have been desensitized toward violence and believe violence is the answer to their problems.

Without aggressive accountability and discipline measures in place, we are destined to fail our students in two ways. First, a lack of accountability and discipline permits disruptive behavior to continue in a classroom setting, which in turn prevents all other students from having their full attention on the learning objective; therefore, students have lower grades with higher failure and dropout rates. Second, if the student's discipline is not tough enough or none at all, there is nothing to discourage the student from repeating the wrongdoing or even worse the student is not affected by the lack of or the level of discipline. The student then decides to take his or her actions to the next level, possibly even crossing the line of wrongdoing to criminal activity.

> We now have a young society starting out with juvenile criminal backgrounds, which is preventing good job opportunities and creating an endless cycle of crime and poverty. What is the price of safety? Without accountability and discipline we cannot have safety or a successful learning environment, and that is priceless.
>
> —Jimmy Sikes, Mesquite Police Department, Mesquite, Texas

The schoolyard fight is another image that seems to typify the schooling experience. Two students meeting after school or during recess to slug it out over some transgression is a pervasive image in American media, especially television and film. But this romantic pugilism is a far cry from the daily reality. While the majority of school violence consists of minor physical conflicts, such conflicts still threaten the safe atmosphere of a school and the learning environment. It's difficult to focus on your geometry lesson when the threat of a physical altercation looms over your head. Similarly, verbal threats are more prevalent than actual physical violence and yet they are just as damaging to the learning environment.

So even if schools were merely facing the romanticized schoolyard fights, that alone would be a detraction and distraction for our learning environments. Yet, as we all know, the types of violence schools face in the present day are not so benign. Fights and confrontations are often not simply on a one-to-one scale, rather they involve groups and gangs. Weapons, drugs, dating violence, and bullying are all major threats to the physical safety of our students.

The container model school can't keep out all the negative influences of the outside world. Our schools are a reflection of the world at large and our students bring those issues with them. How we control those negative issues is paramount. That is where the benefits of a brain-compatible, holistic education come in. The structure of a natural learning, container-model school helps alleviate some of the violence from within.

Emphasizing personalization over standardization will be key to keeping students connected to learning and to people. This emphasis on connecting people with one another and fostering relationships can help ensure a safer environment in two ways: (1) students will be more likely to report a threat, and (2) potential threats can be more readily identified and prevented. Experts report that a healthy school culture can prevent such incidents and even lead students to tell adults about classmates who display warning signs that they could commit such violence. Conversely, standardization leads to depersonalization, which, in turn, leads to disconnect. This disconnection can lead to isolation and hopelessness.

Bill Bond is a school safety specialist at the National Association of Secondary School Principals (NASSP). He was the principal at Heath High School in West Paducah in 1997 when a fourteen-year-old freshman fired on a prayer group, killing three female students and wounding five. Mr. Bond stated in a 2012 interview with NPR shortly after the Sandy Hook shooting at Newtown:

> It's a problem that can be solved with more caring. I don't think it's a problem that can be solved with more security. We've made huge strides with cameras and lockdown procedures. But I can't think of anything at Sandy Hook that would have made a difference. All of our security is based on how we can deter a person because our force is greater than your force and we will ultimately imprison you or we will even kill you. But that's not a deterrent to people, the in-school shootings. So, your normal deterrents, what people think is normal deterrents, have no effect on this. (Martin, 2012)

The same keys to physical safety will also aid in the emotional and psychological safety of our students, faculty, and staff. Neither exists in a vacuum, rather these two needs are reciprocal—feeding off of one another.

Emotional Safety

The physical threats affect our emotional safety. These major events create a sense of fear that must likewise be addressed and alleviated.

Taking care of the physical safety will bolster the emotional safety; however, there are other threats to emotional safety that aren't offshoots of the physical threats.

Maslow's hierarchy once again alludes to this. Once the basic physical needs are satiated, other, emotional needs become relevant. To foster an environment that facilitates and nurtures learning, exploration, creativity—all those things we said are necessary for twenty-first-century education—the contents within the container must elicit a certain emotional security and sense of academic freedom and safety.

Bullying

The issue of bullying has taken front and center of our national attention. No effective school can exist without confronting this issue. Indeed, bullying not only harms the victims, but it dampens the learning environment and erodes public trust. This phenomenon is more reinforcement for teaching the whole-brain child, for the growth mindset, and for true brain-compatible learning.

Just as Bill Bond stated that caring is the answer for physical safety, so too is it for eradicating bullying. Mere punishment for specific instances isn't enough. Our environment must be wholly redesigned. Indeed, much of modern bullying is social-emotional and psychological in nature, thus is can be mitigated through addressing the same needs we highlighted in chapter 2. For example, teaching gratitude, mindfulness, empathy, and other socioemotional learning skills will deliver the most widespread changes on a campus. Thus, time is freed up for educators to really address more individual cases at a deeper level.

The Costs and Benefits

Bolstering safe environments in our schools will also bolster our students' creativity and academic risk-taking; two very important elements of twenty-first-century education. This is an uphill battle that will take time. It is a shift of mind, for the dynamic of holding people down and mocking them for academic achievement is deep with our cultural DNA. It's the stereotypical nerd versus the popular jock. Even in the 1950s, popular culture demonstrated how being smart wasn't cool. To fully return to greatness, we need to create this safe environment for students and staff. America's greatness isn't in standardization but in innovation.

The price of safety is high; however, much of it can be achieved with the return to greatness called for in this book. Indeed, much of the money currently being spent on anti-bullying campaigns is not effective. In part, this is due to a piecemeal approach.

The return to greatness requires a holistic, systemic approach. It is an approach that schools cannot tackle alone. Such a transformation cannot occur solely on the backs and budgets of schools alone. It will take time and a concerted, collective effort. While there is hope for such a transformation, a word of caution is prudent. The return to greatness is no panacea, no utopia, however, the shared, collective vision can remedy some of the underlying threats to safety and create the space for creative solutions.

The School Bus—Where It Often Begins and Ends

The yellow school bus has become an American icon. It is a symbol not only of our public schools, but of youth itself. It also symbolizes a sense of opportunity and freedom. It represents a level of autonomy for our children and a letting go by their parents. It is an icon featured heavily in media. From back-to-school advertisements to commercials to television shows and movies, the yellow school bus features prominently in the American psyche. Sadly, it can also embody the daily threats to our students' emotional and physical safety.

Every day across this great land, our children start and end their school day in one of the worst ways—riding the school bus. The classic scene in the 1994 movie *Forrest Gump* is a moving illustration of the issue of emotional safety.

For those who haven't seen the movie, a young version of the movie's protagonist, Forrest Gump, is a new student trying to find a seat on the early 1950s-era school bus. As he uncomfortably walks down the aisle to unfriendly faces looking for an open seat, children successively tell him sternly, "seat's taken!" in their Southern Alabama drawls—even though the seats are clearly open. More recently, the 2011 documentary *Bully* showcased the threats to physical safety with actual footage of a student being punched and insulted on the bus.

Even under the best of circumstances, we all know what a poor environment the school bus is, yet we simply accept it. And this is not the fault of the bus driver. It is a stressful environment not conducive to an effective start or end to a school day. It is bad for our children's brains. Yet, we do little to nothing about it as a whole. Yes, schools address specific bad behaviors when they become aware of them and video surveillance has aided in this, but these are primarily just bandages.

On the whole, the negative dynamic that is the school bus ride is just a reality we accept and view as too minor a thing to really spend much time on. Our attention is focused elsewhere on seemingly bigger issues, like test scores. This is a tragic fallacy. There is a reason we are concluding with this example. Our school transformation can start with the school bus—just as many of our students start their day.

The way a student starts his or her day can set a lasting tone and influence the amount of learning that can happen. Yet, the majority of these factors are outside the educators' control. How much sleep did students get the night before? Are they well fed? How well have they been provided for emotionally? Did they do their homework? Do they come to us from an enrichment-laden environment or a deprived one? While these influences on a child's readiness to learn are beyond our authority, the school bus environment, however, is within our realm.

Indeed, we do have the power to structure a major emotional and physical safety aspect that greatly influences our students' well-being. We have an opportunity to set the tone for the start and conclusion of their time with us. We can control for the primacy and recency effect of their educational day! These are very powerful opportunities that we are letting slip away! Just how well are we taking advantage of this versus just providing the bare minimum? Think of the possibilities for mindfulness and gratitude training. Likewise, once the students arrive at school, what happens then? Do they sit in the cafeteria engaging in gossip, rumors, bullying? Or do they have an opportunity for brain-enriching activities?

We are not advocating for a rigid extension of the normal school day for our return to greatness, but are we missing out on opportunities to have them primed and ready? As we must revamp everything in our container model, brain-compatible school, transportation is another educational factor that is transformed from a logistical means to an end into an opportunity for creativity and growth.

It can be done, too. And it doesn't have to be expensive or flashy. Unfortunately, despite the given anecdotal evidence and the current emphasis on whole-school discipline programs and positive behavioral supports, there is little research on school bus-riding behavior. Of course, this creates a ripe opportunity for new research and development! There is one promising longitudinal study by Putnam, Handler, Ramirez-Platt, and Luiselli (2003) that we would like to conclude with as an example.

In the late 1990s, the researchers set out to look for innovative ways to improve student discipline in public schools. With a focus on systems-based, schoolwide efforts for improving behavior, they created a bus-riding intervention as a collaborative effort between the administration, teachers, students, and bus drivers.

The whole-school intervention included generating a list of safe bus behaviors and clear expectations for students, teaching the bus drivers how to monitor students more effectively, and providing positive reinforcement incentives for individual students and for whole buses. Student referrals and suspensions for bus behavior significantly reduced the first year and maintained for two more years of monitoring.

While there is a dearth of empirical studies on school bus interventions, the results of this study are encouraging. It is a good example of how such a transformation can occur and endure with planning, collaboration, communication, and consistent implementation. Best of all, it can be done with little expenditures; and once the foundation of positive behavior has been laid, it opens the door for more positive, brain-compatible practices to be introduced in the same manner. We cite this study because it illustrates that we don't have to accept the status quo for our students. The school bus can become an icon for greatness, not harassment.

References

Lowen C., Hirsch, L. Waitt, C., Warren, N. (Producers) & Hirsch, L. (Director). (2011). *Bully* [Documentary Film]. United States: Cinereach.

Martin, R. (2012, December 16). Former Kentucky school administrator recalls 1997 shooting. *Weekend Edition. National Public Radio (NPR).* Retrieved from: http://www.npr.org/ 2012/12/16/167374522/former-kentucky-school-administrator-recalls-1997-shooting

Putnam, R. F., Handler, M. W., Ramirez-Platt, C. M., & Luiselli, J. K. (2003). Improving student bus-riding behavior through a whole-school intervention. *Journal of Applied Behavior Analysis, 36*(4), 583–90.

Starky, S., Tisch, S., Finerman, W. (Producers) & Zemeckis, R. (Director). (1994). *Forrest Gump* [Motion Picture]. United States: Paramount Pictures.

Williamson, M. (2013). *A year of miracles: Daily devotions and reflections.* New York, NY: HarperOne.

8
The Return to Greatness

> Unfortunately, the older we become, the more serious we become. Additionally, most humor that encourages laughter has less to do with jokes than it has to do with building relationships. The leader whose goal is to create a school where everyone achieves understands the importance of building and sustaining trust. Consequently, he also understands how laughter contributes to building trust, which can support a healthier school climate.
>
> —Julie Peterson Combs, *The Trust Factor*

It's complicating! It's messy! It's difficult! It's absolutely necessary! For our public schools to return to greatness, it will take an immense, concerted, complex, and collective effort. We, as educators, parents, and citizens, will have to harness the latest and greatest information and technology we possess both as an academic discipline and as an industry to return to the greatness of America's educational system. This process will make teaching and learning more complicating than it was in the schools of the past. It will redefine many of the roles educators play in the process for the learner.

Teachers, administrators, and educational leaders must shatter outdated tradition to maintain continuity with the past greatness. Those brave enough to embrace this greatness will become more sophisticated in fostering growth and lifelong learning. This is a dramatic shift from the mechanics of past education. Students will be the absolute center of this process. This renewed greatness hinges on learning that will be more personal than standardized. It will be borne from students taking responsibility for their learning.

The American public school return to greatness will not be easy and will take substantial time and effort on the part of school leaders, educators, communities, and policymakers. If the public education community is serious about improving public schools, it can be done. Indeed, we believe it should be and will be done. Just as racing chariots are driven by thoroughbred horses and not pack mules, the twenty-first-century transformation of education will be driven by harnessing the power of our human potential.

Using this metaphor, our approach involves seven drivers for success, each of which is critical and equally important in our return to greatness. We number them for easy identification purposes and not to indicate level of importance or rank. They are individual but together paint a different picture for the schools of the future. While we have discussed each of them throughout the book, we summarize and reemphasize them here to provide you, the reader, an easy synopsis of our vision for the future:

Driver 1—A school that demonstrates a respect for and an understanding of what made public schools great and the ability to build upon its strengths while transforming its weaknesses.

As Dr. Vornberg discussed in his foreword and we emphasized in chapter 1, a strong system of education was envisioned by Thomas Jefferson and Thomas Mann as a necessary ingredient to the great experiment of that time: democracy. They were advocates for that system being a public system, concluding that it was just too critical to be left to other devices.

Although we do not believe they saw a system of standardization versus individualization, time has certainly demonstrated that standardization may have been adequate for manufacturing in the industrial age but clearly we have demonstrated it is no longer adequate in this new, complex information age.

While we reject an erase-and-replace strategy in our return to greatness, we also believe that the status quo has no status in the American public school of the future. Every part of the education endeavor must be requestioned and reassessed through a new non-Cartesian lens to determine what we can use to build the school of tomorrow. Consider another fallacy of Cartesian and Newtonian influence in the American public school:

> One such Cartesian principle that is prevalent in public schools is one of his four methodological rules for seeking truth and understanding. The rule in sum directed to divide things into as many parts as possible in order to more easily understand them (Descartes, 1950). In fact, the idea was to be applied to all matter. Logically, Descartes concluded, all matter can be subdivided, and through the understanding of its parts we gain an understanding of the whole. Alas, the grounding for our modernist perspective on curriculum. Break it up, explain the parts and at some point understand the whole. This thought, coupled with Newton's vision of a stable and geometrical universe of simple organization offers a specific orientation of science being absolute, the scientific method accounting for all phenomenon and hence the way we believed learning of truth occurred. The mechanistic thinking that so influenced the Cartesian and Newtonian vision does not, however, provide for chaotic or complex order of the universe because such chaos or complexity cannot be explained mathematically. (Jones, 2013, p. 16)

Obsolescence is not an option in our view and neither is throwing the baby out with the bath water. Authentic leaders mapping public education's return to greatness must weed out what is illogical or not working within the traditional school model so that we can harness the power of new technologies and amazing advances in science to the school of tomorrow. Our students and our stakeholders deserve no less and are counting on us to figure it out. Education is not a zero-sum game, yet we are competing for our survival and must reverse the trend in marketshare.

Driver 2—A school that reflects a deep understanding and celebration of how America has changed in complexity, demographics, economics, and social structures.

No one thought that Kodak and camera film would become obsolete. No one thought General Motors would declare bankruptcy. No one thought the video tapes and cassette tapes would have no value at a garage sale. No one hopefully thinks American public schools will die. The truth is our world (including education) is changing and growing demographically, economically, socially, and in its complexity faster than many of our most precious institutions have been able to adapt.

Technology has rapidly advanced the influx of new information to the world and our country in all of these areas. Many examples of these realities have been explored in this book. While many things in education have changed since *A Nation at Risk*, much has remained the same even though new discoveries and technology have made them obsolete.

What we understand about the world today requires a new perceptual orientation of learning and learners and far removed from our agrarian, industrial age perspective. This new orientation cannot just be simple semantics like "learner-centered," "multiple learning-styles," or any of the plethora of new language we have created in education only to continue the same old practices of yesterday. This is not window dressing. We talk in schools about being "learner-centered" and then send students to classroom that are almost exclusively "teacher-centered."

Student-centered means individualized and student-directed. It must be as unique as the individual student's brain and mind. It must build on what is already stirring in that individual's thinking. Multiple learning styles mean changing the way you teach based on the style of the learner. It does not mean you reteach that child with a second traditional method. It must be learning that has been individualized and not learning that has been standardized.

Standardization does not develop the individual child, and our return to greatness must do that. Most countries around the world that are outperforming the United States in reading, math, and science have schools that have become less standardized and more individualized—their perceptual orientation has changed for school. We have to become better at personalizing the learning in our quest to develop the individual child's human potential.

The change is about people, not programs. We can still measure student progress with a standardized, formative assessment. That measure can then be utilized as part of a comprehensive accountability system without making the process of learning standardized. Learning must be individual and personal for the learning to be relevant and penetrate the long-term memory.

Learners often understand the trunk without every understanding its part of an elephant. We must harness the traditional practices that keep schools from improving so that we can unleash the amazing new sciences, technologies in neuroscience, postmodern pedagogy, and meaningful and relevant learning designed for individual human potential.

Driver 3—A school that embraces, engages, responds, and reacts to criticism and attacks, both political and social, by the various stakeholders of the school.

Professional educators (administrators, teachers, counselors, and such) must become more empowering of the consumers we serve to eliminate the "us and them" mentality that seems to have us at war. We treat our stakeholders as passive irritants when the truth is these are their schools, their money, and their children. We are simply one of the stewards of these precious resources. We must become responsive to their needs and criticisms and empowering of their involvement but also more engaging and active in their processes and systems of governance. We are all cogs in the wheel of learning (and not at war) but not the wheel itself as educators have traditionally been in the traditional school.

Like private and charter schools, we must compete for our students. Competing means providing a service that is both needed and valued and perceived as being the best option. Is our school the best option?

American public schools' return to greatness can only happen if our stakeholders and our communities think we are great. They need to once again believe that the local public school is the best option for giving their children a leg up when they enter the adult world.

We need our stakeholders to have the same perception of our value and quality that most private schools enjoy from their constituencies. Ultimately, we must harness the attitude of isolation among educators from our stakeholders to unleash the vast opportunities when we partner, empower, and share the responsibility of learning.

Driver 4—A school that encourages and self-directs a comprehensive system of accountability and improvement.

There is a great deal of hostility about accountability among educators and there has been since its beginnings. The unfortunate truth is that for more than a hundred years there was practically no accountability for student performance in public education. In fact, there was little accountability. The result of the accountability movement stemming from *A Nation at Risk* is a system of atonement instead of a system of accountability.

Our need for atonement of days gone by has manifested itself into a system existing in a pressure cooker where instead of no accountability we have pressurized accountability. Instead of using assessment and other school performance data for accountability, responsibility, and meaningful change, our system uses it as punishment and to blame anyone but ourselves.

When we blame we prevent change. Everyone in the system gets his or her defenses up and the chance of self-reflection and meaningful improvement diminishes. Accountability in our return to greatness must be more comprehensive and inclusive as we use meaningful data to improve instruction and help learners reach their individual potential. Blaming the parents or teachers of a prior year or school brings us no closer to that critical objective.

Schools and educators must harness the negativity and fear of accountability and unleash the opportunity to be part of a better more comprehensive system that encourages excellence and value-added learning.

Driver 5—A school that has overcome the rigid pedagogical paralysis that overwhelms most schools today and instead is indicative of ongoing advanced pedagogical development of teachers and administrators that recognizes the emerging and game-changing advances in the neurosciences.

There is no question that we (educators, scientists, and medical doctors) know exponentially more about the brain and learning than we did just thirty or forty years ago! We also know that teacher preparation and instructional methods and pedagogy used in the classroom have not largely changed in light of all we now know. How can we defend that practice?

While everyone does not agree on every aspect of brain activity and function, what everyone does agree upon (cognitive science) is game-changing for the learner if understood, mastered, and utilized. There is a pedagogical paralysis in American public education, and we have developed a system that resists fundamental change in how we teach and facilitate learners:

> Consider for a moment that many of the basic foundations of the traditional math curriculum (integers, operations, decimals, fractions) are taught in multiple grades sometimes six or seven years in a row. If students learn and authentically apply the concepts the first time they are learned, then why do we need to re-teach them year after year? The same can be said about many of the foundations of the language arts curriculum (parts of speech, sentence structure, types of writing). These are just two small examples of curricular repetition that seemingly make learning inefficient. (Jones 2013, p. 12–13)

Educators continue to defend a practice that requires us to teach the same foundation skill year after year. If we teach it at a developmentally appropriate year, with the requisite skills in place, and teach using methods that penetrate the long-term memory, then we only need to teach it once instead of every year until the student is in high school. Most principals and teachers do not have any training in how the brain works and how learning occurs physiologically. That is insanity!

Our return to greatness is dependent on our mastery and utilization of the latest understandings and technologies in the neurosciences so that our pedagogy is logically aligned. We must harness the tendency to continue using traditional pedagogy that is inadequate, ineffective, or inefficient for permanent learning so that we can unleash the game-changing technologies associated with the brain and natural learning. Students

Voices from the Field

School leaders have the great responsibility of modeling continuous educational growth to train and equip teachers to adopt a growth mindset. Modeling such behaviors evokes an expectation for educators to constantly read and investigate educational literature on best practices in the school setting.

Developing and retaining quality teachers are two of the most effective practices in school improvement. However, one of the greatest ways to improve teaching and learning from the school leader standpoint is to remain visible and participatory in the daily activities. School leaders must make a high priority of observing classes and providing helpful feedback. A pertinent facet of the collaborative process is to affirm teachers when effective teaching is observed. It is amazing to me how a small appreciative comment, letter, or remark can lead to such incredible efforts and contributions.

The reality is that there is a sense of urgency to change the way we approach teaching and learning. The difficulty is that change can be uncomfortable and cumbersome. Yet, with a focus on the students, the change from teacher-centered to student-centered learning is monumental in empowering students to pursue authentic scholarship. Initially, the school leader must clearly know and understand his or her vision for the school. The efforts to fulfill and advance the vision must be evident to the faculty and articulated to the constituents. Trust is a crucial component in change, thus a leader's credibility with the community should be solid.

In creating a healthy and vibrant educational setting, a school leader must make every effort to spend time with teachers in observation and discussion regarding best practices. Honest feedback is crucial to teacher growth; however, the delivery of honest feedback is critically important to understanding and implementation. Sincerity and tact are aspects of leadership not often taught in graduate school or leadership development programs, yet are of great significance to the success of the leader.

Additionally, efforts must be made to create an environment where teachers are comfortable with feedback and encouraged to participate in the conversation. The healthiest environments that I have noticed are those in which observations are welcomed and appreciated. Vibrant school cultures result from teachers working with one another, observing each other, and sharing input and ideas that ultimately strengthen the faculty and community. Educators grow from working with each other in a professional and dynamic work environment.

A key factor in improving a school is to make excellent personnel decisions. Seeking and retaining mission-appropriate teachers is imperative in developing a learning community. Faculty selection and retention begins with having an accurate understanding of the identity of the school. School leaders must also provide the resources and support necessary for teacher improvement. One of the greatest forms of professional development is simply visiting other effective schools. Building a network of quality educators from various school settings has provided monumental opportunities for creativity and innovation. This practice builds collegiality on a larger scale and empowers teachers to think outside of the box.

Communicating the vision and hopes for the community will allow teachers the opportunity to fully understand the expectations, goals, and intended outcomes, thus clearly defining the purpose and mission of the faculty. Teachers that tend to embrace the changes are those who have a strong sense of self-awareness and have a high capacity of adaptability. Understanding oneself and remaining malleable often provide a launch pad for professional growth and development.

The landscape of education is changing and evolving at a rapid pace. Students are in need of a whole new set of skills that must be developed in the formative years. No longer are teachers the gatekeepers of all knowledge. Teachers in classrooms today take on the role of facilitator; one who teaches students how to think, not just what to think.

Teachers of the future must have the creativity to ask open-ended questions that lead to deep discussions and introspection. Students have access to so much, yet are in need of the skills to acquire, decipher, and interpret information. Learning at its highest level comes from synthesizing and generalizing information. It is the great responsibility of the teachers, and ultimately the school leader, to foster a collaborative community dedicated to authentic scholarship.

—Justin Smith,
Second Baptist School of Houston,
Houston, TX

that remember what they have learned do not need to relearn it and achieve a higher level of performance. Many of our global competitors in math, science, and reading understand this and are leading the pack in student performance on international assessments.

What is perhaps worse, even harmful, is that what we know about the brain has clearly proven that some traditional instructional methods still used today actually decrease brain activity in learners! American public schools continue to lag behind these critical advances in neuroscience.

Driver 6—A school that demands highly skilled, innovative, and authentic leadership that recognizes the complex nature of teaching and learning.

There are vast sums of research that document building principals and superintendents as key leaders in school districts with high student performance. This has never been truer than for the American public school return to greatness. This endeavor will require the highest quality leaders—authentic, real, and courageous leaders—to accomplish this enormous task.

Authentic leaders in education must first be exemplary teachers so they can be the chief purveyor of teaching and learning. How can you be a leader of teachers and learning if you do not have a current A game in teaching and learning? Even though we have created the language for principals as chief instructional officers or leaders of learning, the reality is that principals and superintendents are not sophisticated about the latest information environments and pedagogy supports that physiology.

In addition to better technical skills, authentic leaders in our return to greatness will have immense skill in capacity building, collaboration, and planning complex change in perception and operation. These leaders will turn pack mules into thoroughbreds as we chart an enlightened course for education and individual districts and campuses.

Salaries for principals and superintendents have improved greatly over the past twenty years, and the consumers and stakeholders of the public school should expect top-notch, inspiring, and results-oriented leaders to head districts and campuses.

Few schools are any better than their leadership. Our return to greatness will ensure that fact. We should harness the ineffective maintainers of the status quo leaders of current schools to unleash a new vision for our schools and attract authentic leadership for the helm.

Driver 7—A school that embraces and ensures physical, emotional, and intellectual safety.

We can do nothing else in schools if we haven't created a safe environment first; and by *safe*, we mean physically, emotionally, and intellectually safe. Safe from factors within the school environment as well as factors outside that environment. Make no mistake, the cost of this safety is high but it is absolutely imperative for all the reasons Abraham Maslow characterized almost seventy years ago. It is the foundational need of all human beings.

The container model applies to so much of what this book has attempted to develop and convey. Like that model, internal and external boundaries are necessary today to ensure that safe environment. Unlike anytime in the American public school history, issues of safety will either make or break a school's ability to do anything positive for its community.

Leaders and professionals charting our return to greatness understand how high these stakes are and are taking preventive steps to ensure a no-failure approach to campus safety, whether it be a terrorist or a bully. They must harness the fear consuming the public that schools are less safe and they can unleash the opportunities of free learning, thinking, and social development for every student.

The Parting Shot

It is always difficult for an author to come to this point in a book that calls for such overwhelming change in a time that some would say is nearing desperate. What do we say when we have outlined a problem and its solution that will take time or money or other resources, perhaps, beyond some of our readers' capacity or current vision. It is all of our problem. If not you, then who?

We have tried to fairly present the issues and we believe our seven driver *cogito* is the reasonable, responsible, and prudent road map for American public education's return to greatness. It cannot happen all at once or across a state or even a school district. It has to happen school by school facilitated by school leaders and other dedicated professionals and community members that take a stand and have the drive for doing their part in the return to greatness.

The sad truth is that much of the current attacks on public education centers on our inability to change, substantively improve, or even do more than a mediocre job and this is evidenced by the immense increase in the push to change public policy to make it easier and less costly for families to abandon the public school (recall our Everyone Can Go to Harvard Theory). They suggest that school leaders are too complacent and either unwilling or incapable of improving the system so public policy should allow them to take the money that would be spent anyway and let the family choose another option.

While we do not believe every school leader can do what needs to be done, we passionately and wholeheartedly believe that the professional educators of this country are not only capable but want to do what is best for the institution we know as public education. Perhaps they need more tools, training, insights, or help in doing it, but make no mistake that public school professional educators (all of them) have not given their life to the betterment of the children of this country to destroy that system they hold so dear.

The late Edwin H. Friedman (2007) characterized this phenomenon in his amazing book *A Failure of Nerve: Leadership in the Age of the Quick Fix*. Not only was Friedman a systems thinker, he was a student of the human brain and wrote extensively, in his anti-Cartesian and Newtonian manner, how the "reptilian" part of our brain that gives us instinct sometimes conflicts with the "mammalian" part of the brain that forges relationships and organizations and the "cortex" part that is considered the "real" brain that gives us the ability to deep think, philosophically speculate, and solve complex problems.

Friedman further explained that if our instinct thinks we cannot do it because of external forces, past failures, complexity of the job, or our own limitations, then most leaders will have a "failure of nerve" regardless of what the organization, relationships, or logic dictates.

How many educators or educational leaders suffer from *a failure of nerve*? The wagers of the war on education would place the number high while people committed to public education want to believe it is much lower. What seems clear is that educators that are successful in the return to greatness are going to have to have the moral courage to defy the instinctive indications that the task is too much or too difficult.

To succeed, we must look beyond the simplicity of our own individual careers to embrace a larger vision that will outlast that career. Maintaining the status quo to buy time and reach retirement cannot be the practice of the school leader leading us back to greatness. These leaders will have to steer into whatever upcoming challenge confronts them and be satisfied that their efforts not only did not contribute to the problem but actually charted the course of success in our quest.

So to that end, regardless of your journey in our return to greatness, we admire your drive and commitment to make a difference and wish you Godspeed!

References

Friedman, E. H. (2007). *A failure of nerve: Leadership in the age of the quick fix*. New York: Church Publishing Company.

Jones, T. B. (2013). *Education for the human brain: A road map to natural learning in schools*. Lanham, MD: Rowman and Littlefield.

About the Authors

Photograph by Kris Hundt

Timothy B. Jones, EdD, is the principal consultant for the consulting firm that bears his name and former full-time and now adjunct professor. He holds a bachelor's in Political Science and General Business from Stephen F. Austin State University (SFASU) and a master's from the University of Houston at Clear

Lake in Educational Management. In 2000 he completed his Doctor of Education in Educational Leadership, also from SFASU.

Since 1984, Dr. Jones has spent his career in school improvement in the roles of teacher, administrator, professor, and principal consultant. While at the University of Texas at Tyler, he cofounded the Principal and Superintendent Institute, which worked with hundreds of school leaders in school improvement initiatives by partnering with Geoffrey Caine of the Caine Learning Center. His inspiration for the Institute grew from the School-Within-A-School he began at Thomas J. Rusk Middle School in the Nacogdoches Independent School District. The program, *The Silver Team*, utilized brain-compatible learning that concentrated on individualized and self-paced instruction for middle school students across the curriculum. The program was the focus of one installment of *Promising Practices in Texas Education* produced by KLRN, the PBS station in San Antonio and broadcast throughout the United States.

To return to his first love—teaching—Dr. Jones left his administrative practice in 1998 to begin his professoriate career. Since that time, he has authored more than seventy publications and made over 140 presentations, keynotes, and in-services while a senior member of the doctoral faculties at Texas A&M University–Commerce and Sam Houston State University. His first book, *Education for the Human Brain: A Roadmap to Natural Learning in Schools* was released in 2013 to great reviews. He is a past president of both the Texas Council of Professors of Educational Administration (TCPEA) and the SFASU Chapter of Phi Delta Kappa. He also edited the highly regarded *School Leadership Review*.

The Texas Congress of Parents and Teachers bestowed an Honorary Life Membership upon him in 1990, and the Texas House of Representatives flew a Texas flag over the Capital for him "In Recognition of His Dedication and Impact to the Education Community of Texas" on May 29, 2009. Additionally, Dr. Jones was awarded Researcher of the Year by the Texas Council of Professors of Educational Administration in 2013 and Distinguished Alumni by the Clear Creek Independent School District

Education Foundation that same year. He makes his home in Dallas, Texas.

For booking information, please see visit http://timothybjones.net or contact his office info@timothybjones.net.

David C. Barrett, EdD, is a senior field trainer and analyst for the Meadows Center for Preventing Educational Risk (MCPER) at the University of Texas at Austin. He currently serves as the assistant director for the Middle School Matters Institute within MCPER working with middle grades educators across the country to build their capacity to better prepare students for success in high school, college, and beyond. He holds a bachelor's degree in psychology from DePauw University in Greencastle, Indiana, and a master's degree in professional counseling from Texas State University in San Marcos. In 2010, he was graduated from Texas A&M University–Commerce with a doctoral degree in Educational Leadership.

Since 1994, Dr. Barrett has worked with adolescents and families in both therapeutic and educational settings. He has worked to foster growth and development with youth and families in a variety of settings: therapeutic wilderness camps, emergency shelters, street outreach programs, family therapy centers, and public middle schools. He has served as a special education teacher, school counselor, administrator, researcher, and adjunct professor. For the last ten years, Dr. Barrett has researched, developed, and implemented innovative ways of using chess in education to promote self-efficacy, math achievement, and problem solving with students who learn differently. He makes his home in Austin, Texas, and enjoys biking, swimming, gardening, music, and, of course, chess.

www.ingramcontent.com/pod-product-compliance
Lightning Source LLC
Chambersburg PA
CBHW021845220426
43663CB00005B/413